THE ARDEN SHAKESPEARE
General Editor, C. H. HERFORD, LITT.D., *University of Manchester*

TROILUS AND CRESSIDA

EDITED BY
ROBERT METCALF SMITH
PROFESSOR OF ENGLISH
LEHIGH UNIVERSITY

D. C. HEATH AND COMPANY
BOSTON NEW YORK CHICAGO
ATLANTA SAN FRANCISCO DALLAS
LONDON

3 A 2

Printed in the United States of America

GENERAL PREFACE

In this edition of Shakespeare an attempt is made to present the greater plays of the dramatist in their literary aspect, and not merely as material for the study of philology or grammar. Criticism purely verbal and textual has only been included to such an extent as may serve to help the student in the appreciation of the essential poetry. Questions of date and literary history have been fully dealt with in the Introductions, but the larger space has been devoted to the interpretative rather than the matter-of-fact order of scholarship. Æsthetic judgments are never final, but the Editors have attempted to suggest points of view from which the analysis of dramatic motive and dramatic character may be profitably undertaken. In the Notes likewise, while it is hoped that all unfamiliar expressions and allusions have been adequately explained, yet it has been thought even more important to consider the dramatic value of each scene, and the part which it plays in relation to the whole. These general principles are common to the whole series; in detail each Editor is alone responsible for the play or plays that have been intrusted to him.

Every volume of the series has been provided with a Glossary, and Essay upon Metre, and an Index; and Appendices have been added upon points of special interest which could not conveniently be treated in the Introduction or the Notes. The text is based by the several Editors on that of the *Globe* edition.

CONTENTS

INTRODUCTION

1. HISTORY OF THE PLAY

Textual History

The transmission of the text of *Troilus and Cressida* from Shakespeare's pen to the First Folio of 1623 offers some interesting bibliographical and textual problems that still await final solution. Research of recent years, however, has cleared up many of the false assumptions of nineteenth century criticism.

We first learn of the existence of the play from an entry in the Stationers' Register for February 7, 1603.

> "Master Robertes, Entred for his copie in full Court holden this day to print when he hath gotten sufficient aucthoritye for yt. The booke of Troilus and Cresseda as yt is acted by my lord Chamberlens Men" (Arber, III, 226).

This record gives us two important points of external evidence that cannot lightly be set aside: (1) that the play had been written before February 7, 1603, and (2) that it had been acted by Shakespeare's company, the Lord Chamberlain's Men. If it was then being acted, as there is no good reason to doubt, it must have been previously licensed for playing by the Master of the Revels, Edmund Tilney. It is probable that Roberts, who was a printer, not a bookseller, claimed, as in other cases, that the Revels license covered the right to print as well as to perform, but that the *full Court*, which passed on doubtful cases, ruled that Roberts must gain the additional assent of one of the Archbishop's licensers, the Archbishop of Canterbury in 1588 having been granted the power to license the printing of books. (R. Crompton Rhodes, *Shakespeare's First Folio,* 1923, 23–24).

Roberts, so far as we know, never carried out his intention of printing the play. When we consider, however, that only two quartos of the 1603 *Hamlet* are extant, neither of them perfect, we cannot be sure that a *Troilus and Cressida* quarto of 1603 may not turn up some day. If Roberts did not obtain the necessary authority, or print the play, good explanations can be advanced. Queen Elizabeth died on the 24th of the following month of March, and the licensing and printing of books during the early months of King James' ascendency were interrupted. Then came the plague, which not only kept the public theaters closed during the fall and winter of 1603 and part of 1604, but also interfered with publishing ventures. Under these circumstances Roberts would have difficulty in selling his copyright to a publisher. "By 1608 he had no interest in the play, having sold his printing shop in Barbican to William Jaggard." Another explanation offered is that Roberts made the entry merely to prevent anyone else's pirating the play from its owners, the Lord Chamberlain's Men.

At any rate the next record of the play on the Stationers' Register is dated January 28, 1609.

> "Richard Bonion Henry Walleys. Entred for their Copy Vnder thandes of Master Segar deputy to Sir George Bucke and master warden Lownes a booke called the history of Troylus and Cressida" (Arber, III. 400).

From this entry we observe that the play had again been licensed for acting, this time by Sir George Buck who had been given full powers as Master of the Revels only since 1606. The Lord Chamberlain's Men, now the King's Men, therefore, applied for a second acting license between 1606–1608, a procedure which would not have been necessary if the play had not undergone revision, or if the company had already given up the play as a hopeless failure.

The Quarto Text. Following the copyright permission came in due course the quarto of 1609, some copies of which have a variant half-title page and an added preface.

The title page first printed reads:

> The Historie of Troylus and Cresseida. *As it was acted by the Kings Maiesties* seruants at the Globe. *Written by* William Shakespeare. London Imprinted by G. Eld for R. Bonian and H. Walley, and are to be sold at the spred Eagle in Paules Church-yeard, ouer against the great North doore. 1609.

From this title page we have further external evidence to refute the traditional view that *Troilus and Cressida* was never produced on the stage. The first entry for Roberts, as we have seen, reads, *as it is acted,* meaning doubtless, as it was being acted by the Chamberlain's Men in 1602–1603; the second entry of 1609 reads "as it was acted," indicating that it had been acted after the Chamberlain's Men had become the King's Men (May 19, 1603) and also at the public theater, the *Globe.* The variant title, rephrased for book buyers rather than theatergoers, reads:

> The Famous Historie of Troylus *and* Cresseid. *Excellently expressing the beginning* of their loues, with the conceited wooing of *Pandarus* Prince of *Licia.*

The rest of the title page is identical, showing no change in type.[1]

[1] Contrary to the traditional views of Malone and Fleay, bibliographical evidence proves that this title page and accompanying preface are later than the title page bearing mention of the *Globe.* The signature at the bottom of the first page of the text of the play is marked A_2; therefore originally there was only one leaf before it, viz, the title page mentioning the *Globe.* The second title was printed with the preface on a half sheet — two leaves, the second signed •|2 at the bottom of the preface page — the usual sign for additional matter later inserted. Furthermore the running head line *The history of Troylus and Cresseida* corresponds with the first title page, which in turn corresponds with the title in the S. R. entry for Bonion and Walley. Finally the early title bears a watermark like that in the rest of the book; the later title and preface have no watermark. Malone believed that as soon as the booksellers discovered that the play had been performed, they cancelled the preface and its accompanying title page, and inserted the words "As it was acted" on the title page. (See A. W. Pollard's refutation of this view, *Shakespeare Folios and Quartos,* 1909, pp. 77–78; also Henrietta Bartlett's *A Census of Shakespeare's Plays in Quarto,* 1916, p. 114.)

The Quarto Preface. We come now to the most interesting epistle to the reader, which is the only known preface to a Shakespeare play issued during the author's lifetime. It is obviously what would be called today a publishers' blurb, written to urge readers to buy the new play of *Troilus and Cressida* because of its great excellence, as well as that of its author, in *comedy*.

The phrase "neuer stal'd with the Stage, neuer clapper-clawed with the palmes of the vulger" has been interpreted by some critics to mean that the play had never been produced on a stage — a view that is no longer acceptable. In view of the external evidences, it is likely that the play had been produced, but had not proved a popular success, and that the publishers were trying to turn this fact to good account by telling readers how fortunate they were that this play, which was caviare to the general, had escaped the multitude, since there was "no comedy more witty," not even the best comedy of Terence or Plautus. They also go on to congratulate prospective readers that the play had been secured from the "grand possessors." This phrase has been interpreted by some to mean the King's company; by others, Shakespeare's friends of rank who had private transcripts. Lee and others think the phrase indicates that the copy had been stolen, but the simpler inferences are, as Alexander (Library, Fourth Series IX, pp. 276 ff.) suggests, that the passage properly read does not refer simply to this one comedy, but to Shakespeare's plays in general, which were guarded jealously by the Company, but when stolen or released for printing had proved popular with the book-buying public; hence the publishers in offering *Troilus and Cressida* were merely capitalizing the well-established favor of Shakespeare's plays. That the Shakespearean Company henceforth succeeded in keeping their plays from publication is witnessed by no further appearance of a Shakespeare quarto in print until the 1622 Quarto of *Othello*, the year before the First Folio.

The amusing preface gives us other valuable information. (1) It tells us how Elizabethan publishers regarded the play, not as a chronicle play, or a tragedy, but as a comedy. (2) It testifies that the author's comedies were popular with readers as well as with theatergoers, a proof, if proof were needed, that Shakespeare was valued in his own day. (3) It reveals that this quarto and doubtless other quartos commonly sold for a testerne, or sixpence. (4) It prognosticates in an astonishing way the future scramble for Shakespeare quartos. But not even the imagination of Shakespeare himself could have predicted the amazing increase in monetary value of a *Troilus and Cressida* quarto. There are in existence at this writing fifteen quartos of *Troilus and Cressida* — four with the first title page, eleven with the second title page. Perhaps one of the finest of all Shakespeare quartos extant is the superb uncut *Troilus and Cressida*, with the first title page, which Dr. Rosenbach acquired from the Holford collection at Dorchester House, and now values at $135,000. In three centuries and a quarter the price of the little pamphlet containing Shakespeare's *Troilus and Cressida* has risen from an Elizabethan sixpence, about fifty or sixty cents in present American money, to a respectable small fortune.

The Folio Text. *Troilus and Cressida* was the cause of trouble and irregularity again when the compositors were setting up the play for its second printing in the First Folio of 1623. The editors originally intended it to follow *Romeo and Juliet* in the third section of *Tragedies*, but after three pages had been set up, something went wrong. It is believed that Heming and Condell, the editors, were having trouble over the copyright still held by Henry Walley, the surviving member of the quarto publishing firm. At any rate, as Professor Adams has conclusively shown, the printers, expecting ultimately to continue the play, left a gap (pp. 78–108) and went on with *Julius Cæsar*. Before the end of the book had been reached, *Timon* was selected to fill this gap. After the plays had been printed and the preliminary pages including the *Catalogue* or list of plays, which omits the title of *Troilus and Cressida*, had been run off, the editors decided once more to go ahead with the play. As there was no other place for it, it was inserted in No Man's Land between the Histories and Tragedies, where it remains in unpaged form. The first three pages left over from the first venture bear the title, *The Tragedie of Troylus and Cressida;* the pages set up after the interruption, merely *Troylus and Cressida.* Though the title and first two following headlines call the play a *tragedy*, and the running headlines in the quarto term it a *history*, we may not take either classification as authoritative, for *Cymbeline*, certainly not a tragedy, the folio editors placed as the concluding play of the tragedy section; and the term *history* as used in the quarto title means story, not chronicle history. Copyright difficulties, therefore, finally overcome, seem to have caused these irregularities in the printing of the play for the Folio of 1623.

The Globe Text. The quarto and the folio texts of the play are substantially the same, but their origins and relationship are still highly obscure. The traditional view, which Clark and Wright, the editors of the *Globe*, accept, is that both texts came from a common manuscript, that the folio text was not printed from the quarto, and that the textual differences between them are caused by revisions which the author himself and also a subsequent reviser made. A recent reëxamination of the problem by Alexander leads to the conclusion that the folio text consisted of a quarto text corrected from a manuscript in the possession of the folio editors, Heming and Condell. The folio, generally the better text, restores some passages omitted in the quarto. The quarto has a few improved readings, and supplies some lines omitted in the folio. Alexander thinks that the quarto, and Chambers that the folio, was printed from Shakespeare's manuscript. A modern text, like the *Globe*, reprinted here, draws from both texts, and makes a judicious selection from variant readings.

Date

Troilus and Cressida may be dated 1601 at the earliest, and at the latest, February, 1603. The "prologue arm'd" (Prologue 23) of *Troilus and Cressida* is accepted by modern scholars as a definite reference to Ben Jonson's *Poetaster*, which was produced in 1601. In February of 1603 James Roberts in applying for a license to print Shakespeare's play noted that it had already been acted by his company, the Lord Chamberlain's Men. The year 1602, therefore, is a generally accepted date for the composition of the play.

Sources

The immediate sources from which Shakespeare derived his *Troilus and Cressida* cannot be determined beyond question. There were available Latin, English, and French translations of Homer, Chaucer's *Troilus and Criseyde* (1385), Lydgate's *Troy Book* (1400), Caxton's *Recuyell of the Historyes of Troy* (1474), and numerous Elizabethan versions of the Troy story in poetry, prose-romance, and drama. An exhaustive examination and comparison of these sources by several modern scholars have brought the following generally accepted conclusions: (1) Shakespeare consulted Homer slightly if at all. (2) he did not use Chapman's translation of Homer as earlier critics believed, for the comedy is a dramatization of Caxton's medieval version of the Troy story, not of the Homeric original. Moreover, only certain books of Chapman's translation were available before 1602; the complete work not until 1611. (3) Caxton's *Recuyell*, rather than Lydgate's *Troy Book*, contains the version most closely and fully resembling the play, and therefore if any single work is to be considered a primary source, it is the account which Caxton translated for his *Recuyell* from the French prose work of Raoul le Févre.[1] (4) Chaucer's

[1] Shakespeare may well have consulted Creed's edition of Caxton (1596).

romantic poem probably served as a supplementary source.

Recent studies, however, by Tatlock and Rollins have demonstrated that the tale of Troilus and Cressida was the most popular love story of Elizabethan times. Adams states that between 1559–1599 "records, which are far from complete, show that it had received dramatic handling at least twenty-nine times" before Shakespeare's. Four accounts within a few years of Shakespeare's play may be found in Robert Greene's *Euphues his Censure to Philautus* (1587), in *Willobie His Avisa* (1594), in Thomas Heywood's play *Iron Age* (1596?) and in the play which Dekker and Chettle wrote for Henslowe in April, 1599. The wealth of contemporary material at hand, therefore, gives weight to Lawrence's statement that "Shakespeare would have been familiar with the tale of Cressida if he had never read a line of Chaucer." Moreover, there are such close relations between Heywood's *Iron Age* and Shakespeare's play, that critics believe either that Heywood and Shakespeare consulted in common an earlier play, or that one borrowed from the other — either Shakespeare from Heywood, as Tatlock thinks, or Heywood from Shakespeare, as Chambers contends.

A chart illustrating the growth of the story out of Homeric materials, and an excerpt from Caxton's version, will be found in the appended notes with a more detailed account of source materials, and with passages from Elizabethan literature which illustrate how Cressida was regarded in Shakespeare's day. In the sixteenth century she no longer appears as the piteous lady of Chaucer's romance, but as a byword for faithlessness and harlotry. We may be fairly certain, then, that Shakespeare, as was so often his practice when confronted by the task of writing a play, went to work upon dramatic materials of Troilus and Cressida already at hand, which, as in the case of the old Hamlet play, he revamped and revised during the years from 1601 to 1603.

Stage History

Recorded performances of Shakespeare's *Troilus and Cressida* cannot be discovered in the annals of the British theater until over three hundred years after the early productions, which the Stationers' Register and the first issue of the quarto of 1609 tell us had been acted by Shakespeare's company before and after 1603.

The theme, however, did not disappear entirely from the theaters. In 1679 Dryden followed his successful reworking of Shakespeare's *Antony and Cleopatra* in *All for Love, or The World Well Lost,* with a similar revision of *Troilus and Cressida, or Truth Found too Late.* In his preface Dryden gives a good account of the alterations he thought necessary to transform "that heap of rubbish," as he styles Shakespeare's version, into a *well-made* play. His most important character changes are the elaboration of Andromache, and the radical alteration of Cressida as faithful throughout in her love for Troilus. This reversal, one might say perversion, of the traditional Cressida permitted Dryden to add sentimental heroics to the love scenes, and to write an effective fifth act in which Troilus accuses Cressida of infidelity; Cressida protests her innocence, Diomedes shows Troilus a ring in proof that he has possessed her; thereupon Cressida stabs herself. Troilus is finally convinced of the truth too late; he kills Diomedes, and is himself slain by Achilles. Dryden maintains Cressida's innocence by having Calchas compel Cressida to entice Diomedes in order that father and daughter may escape to Troy. Troilus sees her giving his ring (not a sleeve, as in Shakespeare) to Diomedes, and believes her false. To heighten the contention scenes, Dryden intensifies the strife between Achilles and Ajax, and introduces a prolonged quarrel between Hector and Troilus. To suit the taste of his Restoration listeners he made the Pandarus scenes much more lewd and suggestive than Shakespeare's. They are not at all in keeping with Dryden's conception of a loyal, innocent, and much suffering Cressida in the last act. Dryden's version continued to be produced in the London theaters through the first third of the eighteenth century. An unsuccessful attempt at revival in London was made by Charles Fry in 1907. In December, 1912, the Elizabethan Stage Society, assisted by the Streatham Shakespeare Players under the direction of Mr. William Poel, gave a performance at the King's Hall, Covent Garden:

> The stage was set in tiers, and a tent which corresponded to the wings, served as a hiding place for the sulking, top-booted, yeoman-like Achilles. The Greeks were presented as Elizabethan soldiers, the Trojans in the flamboyant design of Elizabethan masque costume. Patroclus affected a nasty stutter and smoked a diminutive clay pipe; Thersites was dressed as an Elizabethan clown.

Mr. Poel, a pioneer in the effort to present Shakespeare plays as they were originally produced, that is, continuously on an unlocalized, timeless, and unrealistic platform stage, gave an excellent interpretation of Pandarus.

In March, 1922, *Troilus and Cressida* was again produced by the Marlowe Society at Cambridge, a performance which one spectator declared threw a great light on its meaning. It was as if Shakespeare wished to show the disenchanting side of war, with Thersites a running commentary on the heroic period. The expression of beefy stupidity assumed throughout by Ajax was a masterpiece, and gave a splendid point to all the bating which he has to endure, particularly from the sardonic Thersites.

Troilus and Cressida completed in the following year the production at the Old Vic of all of Shakespeare's plays. On November 7, 1923, in celebration of the Tercentenary of the First Folio, Mr. Atkins presented the play in Elizabethan costumes to a distinguished audience with Princess Mary in attendance. The play was so successful that it continued a second week "with good and enthusiastic audiences." Doris Westwood, who played a minor rôle,

states that when memorizing her lines and attending rehearsals she thought the play a bore, but at the end of the performances she confessed it had grown upon her and she had come to love it. (*A Diary of the Old Vic.*, London, 1926, p. 58 ff.)

On the evening of June 17, 1916, *Troilus and Cressida* made its first appearance on an American stage at New Haven under the auspices of the Yale University Dramatic Association. Under the direction of Mr. Edgar M. Woolley the production was staged in a modern manner "which aimed higher than a bare platform stage and lower than the photography of nature in three dimensions and strove to create broad emotionally suggestive effects without demanding too much either of imagination or reality." The program offered the explanation that the players were interpreting the drama frankly as a burlesque, as they believed that Shakespeare's comic irony was intentional.

On April 16, 18, and on June 11, 1927, *Troilus and Cressida* was again played in America by students at Rockford College, Illinois. This noteworthy production was directed by Mr. Edward L. Davison who had taken part in the performance of the Marlowe Society at Cambridge. Over all the barriers of language and convention "the play made its way with sure and stirring effect — Troilus, the young idealist, puzzled by a militant and disintegrating world, had profound significance in these years following the War; the situation fitted into the actual circumstances." (*Shakespeare Association Bulletin*, Dec., 1927.)

These records bearing witness to the recent popularity of *Troilus and Cressida* as an acting play, are more than paralleled if we turn to France and Germany. At the Odéon on March 20, 1912, and again in 1913 the play, translated into French prose by M. Émile Vedel, was presented in eighteen scenes with very effective stage settings (*La Petite Illustration*, 1913). The French reviewers found it a beautiful spectacle, infinitely diverting — a sort of *fresque*, half-burlesque, half-tragic, which

aroused such good-hearted laughter as rarely greets any modern work. It was as though Shakespeare had indulged in an enormous laugh accompanied by a sympathetic pity for the poor human beings we are.

To Germany belongs the credit for the earliest and longest tradition of *Troilus and Cressida* dramatizations in modern times. Beginning with 1898 we can trace in the Shakespeare *Jahrbuch*[1] at least 150 performances up to 1930, given in the principal cities by at least twenty different companies. From these records we may readily conclude that whenever the play has been staged as a tragedy it has proved unsuccessful, but when played as a comedy has met with the same acclaim it has received in England and France. Since 1925 it has sometimes been played more often than *Love's Labour's Lost, Merry Wives, King John,* or *The Tempest,* and in some years, more often than *Macbeth, Julius Cæsar,* or *Richard III.* In 1925 Otto Falckenburg's production, played twenty-four times, was thought by critics well able to stand comparison with any contemporary Shakespearean production.

2. DRAMATIC STRUCTURE

The dramatic structure of *Troilus and Cressida* has been most roundly denounced by the late Brander Matthews:

> In more than half of the piece the love story is allowed to drop out of sight, while we are distracted by a gallimaufry of debates and battles. The play is a patchwork of amorous intrigues, of wrangling oratory and of gladiatorial combats; the final battle scene is puerile, not to call it infantile, and it belongs to a very primitive period of dramatic art. The play is an incoherent and fragmentary jumble, with no unity of action, no continuity of interest, no dominating figure on which we may center our attention. Uninteresting as a whole, it is infrequently interesting in any of its episodes. Dramaturgically it is the least successful of all the plays accredited to Shakespeare; and this is the reason why it long ago vanished

[1] Vols. 35, 36, 41, 53, 57, 61, 64, 65.

from the stage. The deficiency of action and the absence of motive combine to make the drama dull in any actual performance.[1]

A more careful consideration, however, may redeem the play from such a sweeping and hostile judgment. If *Troilus and Cressida* does not possess the structural unities of a "well-made play" according to the Scribe-Pinero formula, it demonstrably has, what is of more value, a carefully worked out thematic and atmospheric unity. As the title asserts, the main plot is not the fight over Helen by the Greeks and Trojans, but the love story which pervades the whole — beginning, middle, and end from (1) Troilus, the infatuated lover of the first scene, (2) Troilus, the disillusioned lover, to (3) Troilus, awakened warrior of the last scene. The secondary plot, the camp-story, is not merely a parallel with no bearing upon the main plot, but emphasizes the same theme, namely, the unmanning of men by their infatuation for wanton women. In the camp Helen is the faithless counterpart of Cressida, as unworthy of the sacrifice made for her as the devotion of Troilus is wasted on Cressida. Throughout, moreover, Shakespeare emphasizes the points of resemblance between the two stories by employing Thersites as a running fire of caustic abuse. Throughout Thersites keeps hammering upon the central idea that the whole argument is "Nothing but lechery! All incontinent varlets!" Hector believes that Helen is not worth the struggle, and even Troilus, blind to his own infatuation, exclaims like Thersites:

> Fools on both sides! Helen must needs be fair
> When with your blood you daily paint her thus (i. 1. 95–96).

We observe that the chieftains, like Troilus, are also warriors of words rather than deeds, that their long harangues are silly sentiments ending only with such obvious platitudes as "Troy in our weakness stands, not in her strength." Their thoughts are preoccupied with

[1] *Shakspere as a Playwright*, pp. 230–231.

amatory rather than military conquests. Paris (iii. i.) does not fight that day because Helen forbids. Andromache and Cassandra cry out to Hector to "unarm." Achilles, entangled in a love affair with Polyxena, a daughter of the enemy king, gives up his decision to fight on receiving a letter from her. Even Æneas exhibits the same sentiment when he states that he could defer the heavy business of state had he such occasion to lie abed as Paris. In the scene in which the Greek warriors salute the wanton Cressida with kisses, Ulysses, though enjoying the opportunity, as roundly condemns the wantonness of Cressida as Thersites condemns the lechery underlying the whole play. All of these minor love intrigues of the warriors are harmonious variations interplaying with the central theme of the love story. In addition to this thematic relationship between the two plots, we see that the resolution of the Troilus plot is dependent upon the lust for Cressida of Diomedes, another lecher of the Greek camp. Pandarus is suffering from an ache in his bones as the result of his amatory excesses. In view of the skilful working out of theme, tone, and atmosphere, we can hardly accept the view that Shakespeare's artistic genius was asleep when he wrote *Troilus and Cressida*, or that the dramatic structure of the play has no unity of purpose or meaning. The record of many successful performances of the play in recent years, outlined above, bears eloquent witness against Matthews's assertion that it is a dull play which long ago vanished from the stage.

Duration of the Action

As Shakespeare wrote for a non-realistic stage, unhampered by demands for strict chronological time, it is exceedingly doubtful that he laid out his plays according to a calendar of twenty-four hour days. Therefore, the tabular reckonings, which P. A. Daniel worked out so painstakingly for the action of each Shakespeare play, contain inevitable discrepancies. Shakespeare was interested not in clock time, but in imaginative or *dramatic* time. He is careful only to convince his audience that adequate, if unmeasured, time is passing for the course of the action. For example, if we apply the clock test to *Othello*, we find that the events could not possibly have taken place in the time allowed, but by his magic way of suggesting the passage of time, the poet creates the illusion of undetermined intervals and periods sufficient for the success of Iago's prolonged intrigue, so that we never think of raising the question of actual time at all.

According to Daniel, *Troilus and Cressida* consumes four days, though there are discrepancies in Act II, Sc. 3, and Act III, Sc. 1 and 3 that prevent a completely convincing distribution.

DAY 1. Act I, sc. 1 and 2. Interval.'
DAY 2. Act I, sc. 3; Act II and Act III.
DAY 3. Act IV; Act V, sc. 1 and 2.
DAY 4. Act V, sc. 3–10.

3. LANGUAGE, AUTHORSHIP, AND STYLE

Troilus and Cressida has not been neglected by the disintegrators of Shakespeare's texts. Upon the doubtful grounds of a few stylistic differences that they discern in certain passages they contend that the work of other dramatists can be discovered in the play. Fleay (1874) discovered three styles evincing that Shakespeare wrote parts of it at successive periods from 1594–1607; in 1886 Fleay changed his mind in favor of an early play by Shakespeare, and another about 1593 with a subsequent revision by Shakespeare in 1602. Boyle (1901) believed Marston wrote the last two acts, and the prologue and the epilogue. Small (1899) also discerned non-Shakespearean passages. Robertson (1917) contended that the highly Latinized language, and the many unusual words, especially with such terminations as *ion, ure, ive, ate, ance,* characteristic of plays near the date 1602, were evidences of Chapman's hand in the play. These conflicting views, which are destructive of one another, have not been generally accepted. They are based on *a priori* assumptions by the critic as to what Shakespeare's style is, and on the rejection of any passages that do not reach the critic's standard, or that are personally distasteful to him. It is safer to believe that Shakespeare wrote in many styles, good, bad, and indifferent according to his moods, and also according to the requirements of the tone, the themes, the characters, and the purpose of his play. His known versatility should make us hesitate to deny to him any lines in *Troilus and Cressida*, even the prologue and the epilogue which most frequently have been ascribed to another, and yet are in full accord with the intent and tone of the play.

The style of *Troilus and Cressida* has been for critics a puzzle only second to that of the play itself. On the one hand are passages which for splendor of imagery and majesty of cadence it would be hard to surpass and futile to deny as the master poet Shakespeare's very own. On the other hand, if we compare the play with *Hamlet*, the brilliance of style seems wasted upon such a relative paucity of thought. The artificiality, the shallowness of the characters so deprive them of our sympathy and interest that we cannot take with full seriousness the high-flown speeches they deliver. As Wells neatly summarizes the difficulties:

> At least three views are possible in the interpretation of the heroic harangues of Ulysses, Nestor, and Agamemnon: two extreme positions and a moderate one. We may, with several critics, hold that Ulysses voices the sentiments of the poet himself, and take both his ideas and his manner in complete seriousness. We may conceivably hold the speeches so elaborate as to be deliberately burlesque. These are the extreme views. If a moderate position is preferred we shall believe that the poet is in fact sincere so far as the surface glamor of style and imagery is concerned, and even sincere in approving the general purport of the ideas, but that in his judgment of character and of the intellectual background of the scenes, he finds the speakers absurd and their entire outlook on life ridiculous. Shakespeare may well have applauded Ulysses

as a magician in words while despising him as a thinker, as a man, and even as a serious artist.[1]

4. INTERPRETATIONS

After *Hamlet,* the play of *Troilus and Cressida* may be regarded as the most difficult to interpret of all of Shakespeare's plays. Coleridge thought it the hardest to characterize. Written and accepted as a comedy in Shakespeare's day, it has been traditionally viewed in criticism as a tragedy, or as a serious "problem" comedy. Critics of the play may be divided for convenience into four schools: (*a*) the didactic, (*b*) the autobiographical, (*c*) the topical, and (*d*) the historical.

(*a*) The didactic school believes that a dramatist writes plays to expound a philosophy or to inculcate moral teachings. It assumes that Shakespeare wrote his dramas in order to disclose his own philosophical reflections and opinions. *Troilus and Cressida,* when scrutinized for such inner meanings, is susceptible of a bewildering and infinite variety. We need cite here but two interpretations of this kind, one of the earliest, by Ulrici (1876), and the latest by G. Wilson Knight (1930). Ulrici thinks Shakespeare wrote the play to reveal the moral blemish and defects of Greek civilization in contrast with the pristine virtues of Christianity, and to warn Elizabethans of the deep schism in religious and moral life which must come as soon as the people became captivated with Greek culture. Knight, the most recent critic of this school, in his metaphysical essay on the *Philosophy of Troilus and Cressida* contends that Shakespeare is illustrating "the intuition and intelligence opposition" — the Love theme, romantic faith, in struggle with War, cynical intellect — the Trojans standing for "human beauty and worth," the Greeks for "the bestial and stupid elements of man." Many other ingenious interpretations of this sort may be found in other critics of this school — all of them at

[1] Dr. Henry W. Wells has kindly allowed me to quote this passage from his unpublished manuscript on Shakespeare's style.

variance with and destructive of one another. Any thoughtful reader of the play can work out for himself similar schemes and significances of his own if he wishes to ponder upon the sententious passages of the play regardless of its meaning as drama to an Elizabethan audience.

(*b*) The autobiographical school is bent upon viewing *Troilus and Cressida* as the inner revelation of Shakespeare's own soul. George Brandes, the Danish critic, in *William Shakespeare,* and Frank Harris in *The Man Shakespeare* are typical representatives of this kind of interpretation. According to them Shakespeare's plays are "true confessions" in which the poet exhibits to the world the bleeding pageant of his own heart. In the early years of the new century when *Troilus* was written there ensued a period of melancholy in Shakespeare's life, and his soul imbibed poison from everything; he railed against the disillusions of life and perversely revelled in contempt for mankind. "Never had he been so downcast and dispirited, never had he felt so keenly the emptiness of life." *Troilus and Cressida* is the expression of this disillusion. Going further into highly fantastic biographical conjectures, Harris sees Cressida as Shakespeare's faithless lady-love, Mary Fitton, and the poet as pouring out his rancour against her and his rival poet, Chapman. This kind of interpretation braves the great dangers of identifying Shakespeare's own personality with the imaginative creations of his plays. Yet many noted critics entertain it, or lapse into it. Even as objective a critic as Chambers writes, "In *Troilus and Cressida* a disillusioned Shakespeare turns back upon his own former ideals of heroism and romance and questions them." Similarly Tucker Brooke writes, "These two lovers made special appeal to a dramatist who in the period of *Hamlet* and *Troilus and Cressida,* had lost his joy in successful people." Boas, who has written the best character analyses of the play, says, "Only in a mood of the bitterest disenchantment with the world could such a character [Thersites] have been conceived." Lawrence, however, has recently given reasons for believing that there is little connection between Shakespeare's plays and his personal moods and opinions.

(*c*) The topical school believes that the play, or a portion of it, is a veiled satire or allegory of contemporary events. Some critics find references to Shakespeare's rival dramatists, and *The Wars of the Theatres;* others to political events which took place during the early years of the century. According to the first view, Ajax represents Jonson, and Thersites is Dekker — other critics say Marston; the "physic" given "to the great Myrmidon," Achilles (i, 3, 378; ii, 3, 34) is the "purge" administered by Shakespeare to Jonson, referred to in *The Return from Parnassus.* The phrase "rank Thersites with his mastic jaws" is supposed to refer to Dekker's *Satiromastix* (1601). In *Histriomastix* (1599) by Marston and others occurs a dialogue between Troilus and Cressida with the line "When he *Shakes* his furious *Speare*," which is said to refer to Shakespeare's play, though the date, and the frequent occurrences in drama of *shake* and *spear* together in a line, give this view little weight.

Wallace advances the theory that Ajax is Kempe, the former jester of the Globe Company, who after a return from Rome had joined Henslowe's rival company at the Rose. A full knowledge of contemporary history, he thinks, would clear up much of the local allusion, which relates not to the Blackfriars theater quarrel referred to above, but to that between the men of the Globe and the Rose over Kempe's transfer of allegiance.

Acheson brings forward another untenable theory that Shakespeare wrote the play as a splenetic attack upon Chapman, who in publishing parts of his translation of Homer (1597) had championed the Greek heroes.

Tucker Brooke imagines that "Shakespeare, is however subconsciously anatomising the England of the dying Elizabeth: within the walls the febrile Essex type of decadent chivalry; without, the strident go-getters of the new dispensation: Cecil — Ulysses and Ralegh — Diomedes . . . that he sensed in Thersites the lowering shadow of

Prynne and the iconoclasts, and foresaw in Pandarus the portent of the scandalous Carr, Earl of Somerset."

Though there are in Shakespeare's plays indubitable occasional references to contemporary theatrical and political events, as, for example, in Hamlet's conversations with the players and with Rosencrantz and Guildenstern, it is doubtful whether the topical school of critics will be able to work out historical parallels and allegories upon which they can agree among themselves, much less convince others that Shakespeare wrote with any such dominant purpose in mind.

(*d*) The historical school endeavors to discover what *Troilus and Cressida* meant to the theatergoing public of Shakespeare's day, and by inference what Shakespeare intended to do when he wrote the play as a stage production for his company. These critics believe that Shakespeare's principal object as a dramatist was not to expound philosophy, nor to write confession, not to allegorize contemporary events, but to write a successful play. From this point of view Shakespeare's *Troilus and Cressida* was not a popular success like *Hamlet* or other tragedies of this period. Its mood falls short of the high seriousness demanded of tragedy; it does not move to pity or terror, nor has it any characters that arouse our admiration, or command our loyalty or affection. On the other hand, certain passages in the love story and in the war story are too serious for a sustained mood of comedy. The characterization of the warriors, however, is anything but heroic — both Trojans and Greeks are fools — and throughout the drama the principals of both the love story and the war story are subjected to repeated and scurrilous ridicule by Pandarus and Thersites, who act as a chorus of devastating but witty rebuke. The difficulties of classifying *Troilus and Cressida*, therefore, are obvious. Charles Fry who in 1907 produced the play in London, gave the best answer to Tatlock's question as to whether it should be called a tragedy, a history, or a comedy: "Just a play." The Elizabethans were not like critics, sticklers for rigid classification. Moreover, when we consider that Shakespeare in tragedy and comedy alike continually mixed countless moods grave and gay, as for example, in *Romeo and Juliet*, which ranges all the way from the smutty talk of the Capulet servants opening the play, to the romantic raptures of the balcony scene, we need not be surprised to find in *Troilus and Cressida* a few soulful love passages in the midst of some of the foulest raillery that was ever introduced into a play. Though the Elizabethans enjoyed these sharp contrasts, it is obvious why *Troilus and Cressida* did not attain popular success either at the court or at the Globe. The open obscenity of Thersites and the innuendo of Pandarus could not have been delivered in the presence of either Elizabeth or James. In spite of the latitude in talk and jest the court was not like that of Charles II's, but maintained a social decorum above the indulgences of *Troilus and Cressida.* Similarly the play has little appeal for a Globe audience. There are no thrilling melodramatic scenes with which the tragedies are replete; it is a play depending for its effects more upon speech than action, and the references both historical and comical are suited not to a general but to a specialized audience. It would, therefore, never be "clapper-clawd with the palmes of the vulger," nor "sullied with the smoaky breath of the multitude." Alexander has made the pertinent suggestion that Shakespeare wrote *Troilus and Cressida* for the law students at the Inns of Court — just as he wrote *Midsummer Night's Dream* to celebrate the wedding of a noble lord and lady, and the *Merry Wives* for the Queen at the Windsor Christmas festivities. To the law students a broad comedy on the love story of Troilus and Cressida, and the war story as well, would not only be traversing familiar ground, but would be highly entertaining. The students would enjoy the high-flown passages of contention between the Greek and Trojan warriors, as well as the few lyrical interchanges between the lovers. Who can doubt that the innuendo of Pandarus and the raillery of Thersites would be greeted by them, not with indignation or resentment, but with "inextinguishable laughter"? Many critics, however, have found the speeches of Thersites so repellent that they could conceive them only as the utterances of a poet completely disillusioned with life. And here some of the historical critics go astray because they have approached the play still under the spell of Homer's noble characterizations, or Chaucer's romantic and sympathetic delineation of the lovers, and have deeply resented what they deemed Shakespeare's incorrigible degradation of both. The following condemnation from Root, the Chaucer enthusiast and scholar, may serve as representative of those who condemn Shakespeare because he ignored the tradition of Homer and Chaucer, or because he did not, as Henryson did, and as Dryden and Rollins demand that he should have done — punish Cressida in order to satisfy morality and poetic justice.

> If Chaucer has transformed the spirit of the story from pathetic sentimentality to half-ironical humor, Shakespeare, in his *Troilus and Cressida*, has approached it in a spirit of bitter cynicism and blackest pessimism. The love story, which is after all subordinate to the intrigues of the Grecian camp, has neither the romance of Boccaccio nor the humor of Chaucer; it is merely disgusting. Troilus remains much what he is in Chaucer; but Cressida has flung away even the pretense of virtue, and is merely a confessed wanton. The keen-sighted Ulysses reads her at a glance: —
>
> "Fie, fie upon her!
> There's language in her eye, her cheek, her lip,
> Nay, her foot speaks; her wanton spirits look out
> At every joint and motive of her body.
> O, these encounterers, so glib of tongue,
> That give accosting welcome ere it comes,
> And wide unclasp the tables of their thoughts
> To every ticklish reader! set them down
> For sluttish spoils of opportunity,
> And daughters of the game" (iv. 5. 54–63).
>
> That the generous Troilus, own brother of Romeo, should break his heart for such a woman as this is but another proof of the essential mockery of human life. Pandarus has lost

all his geniality and humor, and is merely repulsive. To crown all, the final worthlessness of Cressida, and the breaking heart of Troilus, are interpreted to us by the syphilitic mind of Thersites, whose whole function in the play is to defile with the foulness of his own imagination all that humanity holds high and sacred.

Structurally as well as spiritually the play is bad, redeemed only by a few noble speeches in the Grecian camp; and it remains one of the puzzles of criticism that such a work should ever have proceeded from the great soul of Shakespeare. (*The Poetry of Chaucer*, 1922, pp. 99–100.)

To absolve Shakespeare from this diatribe we need only to remember that his interpretation was not original in substance, but merely that popularly known to his fellow Elizabethans. Long before Shakespeare thought of dramatizing the story, the Greeks and Trojans had lost their heroic glamour. Paris and Troilus had become love-sick swains, and Helen and Cressida notorious wantons, ripe for the genius of Shakespeare to take them off with the devastating ridicule of Pandarus and Thersites. For proof let the teacher read aloud to a class of college men one of several masterpieces of abuse given by Shakespeare to Thersites, the uncrowned and unconquered king of railers, and he will be greeted with the same kind of laughter that the Thersites of the King's Men would have aroused at the Inns of Court.[1] Moreover, the insistent praise of the play in the quarto preface, as a comedy comparable in wit with the plays of Plautus and Terence, should, it would seem, clinch the question as to how the play was conceived by the author and interpreted by publishers, playgoers, and readers in Shakespeare's day. To interpret the talk of Pandarus and Thersites as proceeding from "bitter cynicism and blackest pessimism" is, therefore, to be blind to one aspect of Shakespeare's comic muse. "It is impossible to believe Shakespeare so naïve as to be wholly

[1] Alexander (*Library*, Fourth Series, IX, p. 278) and Adams (*Life of Shakespeare*, p. 210) show how Shakespeare's company often assisted at hilarious revels at the Inns of Court.

taken in by his own creations; and an insult to his intelligence to hold that he could write throughout such inflated and verbose speeches without some provocation of the spirit of comedy." As Guha remarks, if we could change the names, and forget what Achilles was in Homer, and Cressida in Chaucer, we should realize that we have in Shakespeare's play a witty comedy on *Much Ado About Women*.

Viewed, then, as a broad comedy written to arouse Homeric laughter among the law students, the alternation of heroic, mock heroic, and scandalously ridiculous sentiments is not incompatible with Shakespeare's practice, but is the very stuff of comedy itself. If the play seems too sardonic for our taste, which prefers what Taylor has called the "milk-and-water diet" of Shaw's *Cæsar and Cleopatra*, and Erskine's *Private Life of Helen of Troy*, we have ample evidence in the preface of 1609 that the publishers knew their readers were not afflicted with any such squeamishness.

Stapfer, as long ago as 1880, came to similar conclusions when he wrote:

> *Troilus and Cressida* is, to sum up, the playful recreation with which a great genius amused himself in his lighter moods, when, finding in the traditions of the two lovers and of the Trojan war a framework that struck his fancy, he filled it up, somewhat hastily indeed, but lavishing upon it all he has taught us to expect from him, of dramatic life and wealth of ideas, of wit, of pathos and of poetry. To seek for any deep hidden meaning in this play implies an utter misconception of its character. In order to appreciate it, it is necessary to enter into Shakespeare's *humour* and frankly to throw off all literary and moral preconceptions, without pretending to greater seriousness than he did himself. Then our admiration can be freely given to a poet who is so perfectly distinct from all his characters, and is so completely independent and at his ease, moulding his subject after his sovereign will and pleasure and we are of one mind with Goethe when he said to Eckermann, "If you wish to know Shakespeare's utter freedom of thought, read *Troilus and Cressida*."

THE EPISTLE, OR PREFACE TO THE QUARTO

A NEUER WRITER, TO AN EUER READER. NEWES.

Eternall reader, you haue heere a new play, neuer stal'd with the Stage, neuer clapper-clawd with the palmes of the vulger, and yet passing full of the palme comicall; for it is a birth of your braine, that neuer vnder-tooke any thing commicall, vainely: And were but the vaine names of commedies changde for the titles of Commodities, or of Playes for Pleas; you should see all those grand censors, that now stile them such vanities, flock to them for the maine grace of their grauities: especially this authors Commedies, that are so fram'd to the life, that they serue for the most common Commentaries, of all the actions of our liues shewing such a dexteritie, and power of witte, that the most displeased with Playes, are pleasd with his Commedies. And all such dull and heauy-witted worldlings, as were neuer capable of the witte of a Commedie, comming by report of them to his representations, haue found that witte there, that they neuer found in them selues, and haue parted betterwittied then they came: feeling an edge of witte set vpon them, more then euer they dreamed they had braine to grinde it on. So much and such sauored Salt of witte is in his Commedies, that they seeme (for their height of pleasure) to be borne in that sea that brought forth VENUS. Amongst all there is none more witty then this: And had I time I would comment vpon it, though I know it needs not, (for so much as will make you thinke your testerne well bestowd) but for so much worth, as euen poore I know to be stuft in it. It deserues such a labour, as well as the best Commedy in TERENCE or PLAUTUS. And beleeue this, that when hee is gone, and his Commedies out of sale, you will scramble for them, and set vp a new English Inquisition. Take this for a warning, and at the perrill of your pleasures losse, and Iudgements, refuse not, nor like this the lesse, for not being sullied, with the smoaky breath of the multitude; but thanke fortune for the scape it hath made amongst you. Since by the grand possessors wills I beleeue you should haue prayd for them rather then beene prayd. And so I leaue all such to bee prayd for (for the states of their wits healths) that will not praise it. Vale.

TROILUS AND CRESSIDA

DRAMATIS PERSONÆ

PRIAM	King of Troy
HECTOR, TROILUS, PARIS, DEIPHOBUS, HELENUS	His sons
MARGARELON	A bastard son of Priam
ÆNEAS, ANTENOR	Trojan commanders
CALCHAS	A Trojan priest, taking part with the Greeks
PANDARUS	Uncle to Cressida
AGAMEMNON	The Grecian general
MENELAUS	His brother
ACHILLES, AJAX, ULYSSES, NESTOR, DIOMEDES, PATROCLUS	Grecian commanders
THERSITES	A deformed and scurrilous Grecian
ALEXANDER	Servant to Cressida
Servant to Troilus	
Servant to Paris	
Servant to Diomedes	
HELEN	Wife to Menelaus
ANDROMACHE	Wife to Hector
CASSANDRA	Daughter to Priam; a prophetess
CRESSIDA	Daughter to Calchas

Trojan and Greek Soldiers, and Attendants

SCENE — TROY, AND THE GRECIAN CAMP

TROILUS AND CRESSIDA

THE PROLOGUE

In Troy there lies the scene. From isles of Greece
The princes orgulous, their high blood chafed,
Have to the port of Athens sent their ships,
Fraught with the ministers and instruments
Of cruel war: sixty and nine, that wore
Their crownets regal, from the Athenian bay
Put forth toward Phrygia, and their vow is made
To ransack Troy, within whose strong immures
The ravish'd Helen, Menelaus' queen,
With wanton Paris sleeps; and that's the quarrel. 10
To Tenedos they come;
And the deep-drawing barks do there disgorge
Their warlike fraughtage: now on Dardan plains
The fresh and yet unbruised Greeks do pitch
Their brave pavilions: Priam's six-gated city,
Dardan, and Timbria, Helias, Chetas, Troien,
And Antenorides, with massy staples,
And corresponsive and fulfilling bolts,
Sperr up the sons of Troy.
Now expectation, tickling skittish spirits, 20
On one and other side, Trojan and Greek,
Sets all on hazard: and hither am I come
A prologue arm'd, but not in confidence
Of author's pen or actor's voice, but suited
In like conditions as our argument,
To tell you, fair beholders, that our play

Leaps o'er the vaunt and firstlings of those broils,
Beginning in the middle; starting thence away
To what may be digested in a play.
Like, or find fault; do as your pleasures are: 30
Now good or bad, 'tis but the chance of war.

ACT I

Scene I — *Troy. Before Priam's palace*

Enter Pandarus *and* Troilus

Tro. Call here my varlet; I'll unarm again:
Why should I war without the walls of Troy,
That find such cruel battle here within?
Each Trojan that is master of his heart,
Let him to field; Troilus, alas! hath none!

Pan. Will this gear ne'er be mended?

Tro. The Greeks are strong and skilful to their strength,
Fierce to their skill and to their fierceness valiant,
But I am weaker than a woman's tear,
Tamer than sleep, fonder than ignorance, 10
Less valiant than the virgin in the night,
And skilless as unpractised infancy.

Pan. Well, I have told you enough of this: for my part, I'll not meddle nor make no farther. He that will have a cake out of the wheat must needs tarry the grinding.

Tro. Have I not tarried?

Pan. Ay, the grinding; but you must tarry the bolting.

Tro. Have I not tarried? 20

Pan. Ay, the bolting; but you must tarry the leavening.

Tro. Still have I tarried.

Pan. Ay, to the leavening; but here's yet in the word 'hereafter,' the kneading, the making of the cake, the heating of the oven, and the baking; nay, you must stay the cooling too, or you may chance to burn your lips.

Tro. Patience herself, what goddess e'er she be,
Doth lesser blench at sufferance than I do. 30
At Priam's royal table do I sit;
And when fair Cressid comes into my thoughts, —
So, traitor! — 'When she comes!' — When is she
thence?

Pan. Well, she looked yesternight fairer than ever I saw her look, or any woman else.

Tro. I was about to tell thee: — when my heart,
As wedged with a sigh, would rive in twain,
Lest Hector or my father should perceive me,
I have, as when the sun doth light a storm,
Buried this sigh in wrinkle of a smile: 40
But sorrow, that is crouch'd in seeming gladness,
Is like that mirth fate turns to sudden sadness.

Pan. An her hair were not somewhat darker than Helen's — well, go to — there were no more comparison between the women: but, for my part, she is my kinswoman; I would not, as they term it, praise her: but I would somebody had heard her talk yesterday, as I did. I will not dispraise your sister Cassandra's wit, but —

Tro. O Pandarus! I tell thee, Pandarus, — 50

When I do tell thee, there my hopes lie drown'd,
Reply not in how many fathoms deep
They lie indrench'd. I tell thee, I am mad
In Cressid's love: thou answer'st 'she is fair;'
Pour'st in the open ulcer of my heart
Her eyes, her hair, her cheek, her gait, her voice,
Handlest in thy discourse, O, that her hand,
In whose comparison all whites are ink
Writing their own reproach, to whose soft seizure
The cygnet's down is harsh, and spirit of sense 60
Hard as the palm of ploughman: this thou tell'st me,
As true thou tell'st me, when I say I love her;
But, saying thus, instead of oil and balm,
Thou lay'st in every gash that love hath given me
The knife that made it.

Pan. I speak no more than truth.

Tro. Thou dost not speak so much.

Pan. Faith, I'll not meddle in 't. Let her be as she is: if she be fair, 'tis the better for her; an she be not, she has the mends in her own hands. 70

Tro. Good Pandarus, how now, Pandarus!

Pan. I have had my labour for my travail; ill-thought on of her, and ill-thought on of you: gone between and between, but small thanks for my labour.

Tro. What, art thou angry, Pandarus? what, with me?

Pan. Because she's kin to me, therefore she's not so fair as Helen: an she were not kin to me, she would be as fair on Friday as Helen is on Sunday. 80 But what care I? I care not an she were a black-a-moor; 'tis all one to me.

Tro. Say I she is not fair?

Pan. I do not care whether you do or no. She's a fool to stay behind her father; let her to the Greeks; and so I'll tell her the next time I see her: for my part, I'll meddle nor make no more i' the matter.

Tro. Pandarus, —

Pan. Not I. 90

Tro. Sweet Pandarus, —

Pan. Pray you, speak no more to me: I will leave all as I found it, and there an end. [*Exit. An alarum.*

Tro. Peace, you ungracious clamours! peace, rude sounds!
Fools on both sides! Helen must needs be fair,
When with your blood you daily paint her thus.
I cannot fight upon this argument;
It is too starved a subject for my sword.
But Pandarus — O gods, how do you plague me!
I cannot come to Cressid but by Pandar; 100
And he's as tetchy to be woo'd to woo
As she is stubborn-chaste against all suit.
Tell me, Apollo, for thy Daphne's love,
What Cressid is, what Pandar, and what we.
Her bed is India; there she lies, a pearl:
Between our Ilium and where she resides,
Let it be call'd the wild and wandering flood,
Ourself the merchant, and this sailing Pandar
Our doubtful hope, our convoy and our bark.

Alarum. Enter ÆNEAS

Æne. How now, Prince Troilus! wherefore not afield?. 110

Tro. Because not there: this woman's answer sorts,
For womanish it is to be from thence.
What news, Æneas, from the field to-day?
Æne. That Paris is returned home, and hurt.
Tro. By whom, Æneas?
Æne. Troilus, by Menelaus.
Tro. Let Paris bleed: 'tis but a scar to scorn;
Paris is gored with Menelaus' horn. [*Alarum.*
Æne. Hark, what good sport is out of town to-day!
Tro. Better at home, if 'would I might' were 'may.'
But to the sport abroad: are you bound thither? 120
Æne. In all swift haste.
Tro. Come, go we then together.
[*Exeunt.*

SCENE II — *The same. A street*

Enter CRESSIDA *and* ALEXANDER her man

Cres. Who were those went by?
Alex. Queen Hecuba and Helen.
Cres. And whither go they?
Alex. Up to the eastern tower,
Whose height commands as subject all the vale,
To see the battle. Hector, whose patience
Is as a virtue fix'd, to-day was moved:
He chid Andromache and struck his armourer;
And, like as there were husbandry in war,
Before the sun rose he was harness'd light,
And to the field goes he; where every flower
Did, as a prophet, weep what it foresaw 10
In Hector's wrath.

Cres. What was his cause of anger?

Alex. The noise goes, this: there is among the Greeks
A lord of Trojan blood, nephew to Hector;
They call him Ajax.

Cres. Good; and what of him?

Alex. They say he is a very man per se,
And stands alone.

Cres. So do all men, unless they are drunk, sick, or have no legs.

Alex. This man, lady, hath robbed many beasts of their particular additions; he is as valiant as 20 the lion, churlish as the bear, slow as the elephant: a man into whom nature hath so crowded humours that his valour is crushed into folly, his folly sauced with discretion: there is no man hath a virtue that he hath not a glimpse of, nor any man an attaint but he carries some stain of it: he is melancholy without cause and merry against the hair: he hath the joints of every thing; but every thing so out of joint that he is a gouty Briareus, many hands and no use, or pur- 30 blind Argus, all eyes and no sight.

Cres. But how should this man, that makes me smile, make Hector angry?

Alex. They say he yesterday coped Hector in the battle and struck him down, the disdain and shame whereof hath ever since kept Hector fasting and waking.

Enter PANDARUS

Cres. Who comes here?

Alex. Madam, your uncle Pandarus.

Cres. Hector's a gallant man. 40

Alex. As may be in the world, lady.

Pan. What's that? what's that?

Cres. Good morrow, uncle Pandarus.

Pan. Good morrow, cousin Cressid: what do you talk of? Good morrow, Alexander. How do you, cousin? When were you at Ilium?

Cres. This morning, uncle.

Pan. What were you talking of when I came? Was Hector armed and gone ere you came to Ilium? Helen was not up, was she? 50

Cres. Hector was gone; but Helen was not up.

Pan. E'en so: Hector was stirring early.

Cres. That were we talking of, and of his anger.

Pan. Was he angry?

Cres. So he says here.

Pan. True, he was so; I know the cause too; he'll lay about him to-day, I can tell them that; and there's Troilus will not come far behind him; let them take heed of Troilus, I can tell them that too. 60

Cres. What, is he angry too?

Pan. Who, Troilus? Troilus is the better man of the two.

Cres. O Jupiter; there's no comparison.

Pan. What, not between Troilus and Hector? Do you know a man if you see him?

Cres. Ay, if I ever saw him before and knew him.

Pan. Well, I say Troilus is Troilus.

Cres. Then you say as I say; for, I am sure, he is not Hector. 70

Pan. No, nor Hector is not Troilus in some degrees.

Cres. 'Tis just to each of them; he is himself.

Pan. Himself! Alas, poor Troilus! I would he were.

Cres. So he is.

Pan. Condition, I had gone barefoot to India.

Cres. He is not Hector. 80

Pan. Himself! no, he's not himself: would a' were himself! Well, the gods are above; time must friend or end: well, Troilus, well, I would my heart were in her body! No, Hector is not a better man than Troilus.

Cres. Excuse me.

Pan. He is elder.

Cres. Pardon me, pardon me.

Pan. Th' other's not come to 't; you shall tell me another tale, when th' other's come to 't. 90 Hector shall not have his wit this year.

Cres. He shall not need it, if he have his own.

Pan. Nor his qualities.

Cres. No matter.

Pan. Nor his beauty.

Cres. 'Twould not become him; his own's better.

Pan. You have no judgement, niece: Helen herself swore th' other day, that Troilus, for a brown favour — for so 'tis, I must confess, — not 100 brown neither, —

Cres. No, but brown.

Pan. Faith, to say truth, brown and not brown.

Cres. To say the truth, true and not true.

Pan. She praised his complexion above Paris.

Cres. Why, Paris hath colour enough.

Pan. So he has.

Cres. Then Troilus should have too much: if she praised him above, his complexion is higher 110 than his; he having colour enough, and the other higher, is too flaming a praise for a good complexion. I had as lief Helen's golden tongue had commended Troilus for a copper nose.

Pan. I swear to you, I think Helen loves him better than Paris.

Cres. Then she's a merry Greek indeed.

Pan. Nay, I am sure she does. She came to him th' other day into the compassed window, — and, you know, he has not past three or four hairs on 120 his chin, —

Cres. Indeed, a tapster's arithmetic may soon bring his particulars therein to a total.

Pan. Why, he is very young: and yet will he, within three pound, lift as much as his brother Hector.

Cres. Is he so young a man and so old a lifter?

Pan. But, to prove to you that Helen loves him: she came and puts me her white hand to his cloven 130 chin, —

Cres. Juno have mercy! how came it cloven?

Pan. Why, you know, 'tis dimpled: I think his smiling becomes him better than any man in all Phrygia.

Cres. O, he smiles valiantly.

Pan. Does he not?

Cres. O yes, an 'twere a cloud in autumn.

Pan. Why, go to, then: but to prove to you that Helen loves Troilus, — 140

Cres. Troilus will stand to the proof, if you'll prove it so.

Pan. Troilus! why, he esteems her no more than I esteem an addle egg.

Cres. If you love an addle egg as well as you love an idle head, you would eat chickens i' the shell.

Pan. I cannot choose but laugh, to think how she tickled his chin; indeed, she has a marvellous white hand, I must needs confess, — 150

Cres. Without the rack.

Pan. And she takes upon her to spy a white hair on his chin.

Cres. Alas, poor chin! many a wart is richer.

Pan. But there was such laughing! Queen Hecuba laughed, that her eyes ran o'er.

Cres. With mill-stones.

Pan. And Cassandra laughed.

Cres. But there was more temperate fire under the pot of her eyes: did her eyes run o'er too? 160

Pan. And Hector laughed.

Cres. At what was all this laughing?

Pan. Marry, at the white hair that Helen spied on Troilus' chin.

Cres. An't had been a green hair, I should have laughed too.

Pan. They laughed not so much at the hair as at his pretty answer.

Cres. What was his answer?

Pan. Quoth she, 'Here's but two and fifty hairs 170
on your chin, and one of them is white.'

Cres. This is her question.

Pan. That's true; make no question of that.
'Two and fifty hairs,' quoth he, 'and one white:
that white hair is my father, and all the rest are his
sons.' 'Jupiter!' quoth she, 'which of these
hairs is Paris my husband?' 'The forked one,'
quoth he, 'pluck 't out, and give it him.' But
there was such laughing! and Helen so blushed,
and Paris so chafed, and all the rest so laughed, 180
that it passed.

Cres. So let it now; for it has been a great while
going by.

Pan. Well, cousin, I told you a thing yesterday;
think on't.

Cres. So I do.

Pan. I'll be sworn 'tis true; he will weep you,
an 'twere a man born in April.

Cres. And I'll spring up in his tears, an 'twere a
nettle against May. [*A retreat sounded.* 190

Pan. Hark! they are coming from the field:
shall we stand up here and see them as they pass
toward Ilium? good niece, do, sweet niece
Cressida.

Cres. At your pleasure.

Pan. Here, here, here's an excellent place; here
we may see most bravely: I'll tell you them
all by their names as they pass by; but mark
Troilus above the rest.

ÆNEAS *passes*

Cres. Speak not so loud. 200

Pan. That's Æneas: is not that a brave man? he's one of the flowers of Troy, I can tell you: but mark Troilus; you shall see anon.

Cres. Who's that?

ANTENOR *passes*

Pan. That's Antenor: he has a shrewd wit, I can tell you; and he's a man good enough: he's one o' the soundest judgements in Troy, whosoever, and a proper man of person. When comes Troilus? I'll show you Troilus anon: if he see me, you shall see him nod at me. 210

Cres. Will he give you the nod?

Pan. You shall see.

Cres. If he do, the rich shall have more.

HECTOR *passes*

Pan. That's Hector, that, that, look you, that; there's a fellow! Go thy way, Hector! There's a brave man, niece. O brave Hector! Look how he looks! there's a countenance! is't not a brave man?

Cres. O, a brave man!

Pan. Is a' not? it does a man's heart good. 220 Look you what hacks are on his helmet! look you yonder, do you see? look you there: there's no jesting; there's laying on, take 't off who will, as they say: there be hacks!

Cres. Be those with swords?

Pan. Swords! any thing, he cares not; an the

devil come to him, it's all one: by God's lid, it does one's heart good. Yonder comes Paris, yonder comes Paris.

Paris *passes*

Look ye yonder, niece; is 't not a gallant man 230 too, is 't not? Why, this is brave now. Who said he came hurt home to-day? he's not hurt: why, this will do Helen's heart good now, ha! Would I could see Troilus now! you shall see Troilus anon.

Cres. Who's that?

Helenus *passes*

Pan. That's Helenus: I marvel where Troilus is. That's Helenus. I think he went not forth to-day. That's Helenus.

Cres. Can Helenus fight, uncle? 240

Pan. Helenus! no; yes, he'll fight indifferent well. I marvel where Troilus is. Hark! do you not hear the people cry 'Troilus'? Helenus is a priest.

Cres. What sneaking fellow comes yonder?

Troilus *passes*

Pan. Where? yonder? that's Deiphobus. 'Tis Troilus! there's a man, niece! Hem! Brave Troilus! the prince of chivalry!

Cres. Peace, for shame, peace!

Pan. Mark him; note him. O brave Troilus! 250 Look well upon him, niece; look you how his sword is bloodied, and his helm more hacked than Hector's; and how he looks, and how he goes! O admirable youth! he never saw three-and-twenty. Go thy way, Troilus, go thy way! Had I a sister were a grace, or a daughter a goddess, he should take his choice. O admirable man! Paris? Paris is dirt to him; and, I warrant, Helen, to change, would give an eye to boot.

Common Soldiers *pass*

Cres. Here come more. 260

Pan. Asses, fools, dolts! chaff and bran, chaff and bran! porridge after meat! I could live and die i' the eyes of Troilus. Ne'er look, ne'er look; the eagles are gone: crows and daws, crows and daws! I had rather be such a man as Troilus than Agamemnon and all Greece.

Cres. There is among the Greeks Achilles, a better man than Troilus.

Pan. Achilles! a drayman, a porter, a very camel. 270

Cres. Well, well.

Pan. Well, well! Why, have you any discretion? have you any eyes? do you know what a man is? Is not birth, beauty, good shape, discourse, manhood, learning, gentleness, virtue, youth, liberality, and such like, the spice and salt that season a man?

Cres. Ay, a minced man: and then to be baked with no date in the pie, for then the man's date is out. 280

Pan. You are such a woman! one knows not at what ward you lie.

Cres. Upon my back, to defend my belly; upon

my wit, to defend my wiles; upon my secrecy, to defend mine honesty; my mask, to defend my beauty; and you, to defend all these: and at all these wards I lie, at a thousand watches.

Pan. Say one of your watches.

Cres. Nay, I'll watch you for that; and that's one of the chiefest of them too: if I cannot ward what I would not have hit, I can watch you for telling how I took the blow; unless it swell past hiding, and then it's past watching. 290

Pan. You are such another!

Enter Troilus's Boy

Boy. Sir, my lord would instantly speak with you.

Pan. Where?

Boy. At your own house; there he unarms him.

Pan. Good boy, tell him I come. [*Exit Boy.*] I doubt he be hurt. Fare ye well, good niece. 300

Cres. Adieu, uncle.

Pan. I will be with you, niece, by and by.

Cres. To bring, uncle?

Pan. Ay, a token from Troilus.

Cres. By the same token, you are a bawd.

[*Exeunt Pandarus.*

Words, vows, gifts, tears, and love's full sacrifice,
He offers in another's enterprise:
But more in Troilus thousand fold I see
Than in the glass of Pandar's praise may be; 310
Yet hold I off. Women are angels, wooing:
Things won are done; joy's soul lies in the doing:

That she beloved knows nought that knows not this:
Men prize the thing ungain'd more than it is:
That she was never yet that ever knew
Love got so sweet as when desire did sue:
Therefore this maxim out of love I teach:
Achievement is command; ungain'd, beseech.
Then though my heart's content firm love doth bear,
Nothing of that shall from mine eyes appear. 320
[*Exeunt.*

SCENE III — *The Grecian camp. Before Agamemnon's tent*

Sennet. Enter AGAMEMNON, NESTOR, ULYSSES, MENELAUS, *with others*

Agam. Princes,
What grief hath set the jaundice on your cheeks?
The ample proposition that hope makes
In all designs begun on earth below
Fails in the promised largeness: checks and disasters
Grow in the veins of actions highest rear'd,
As knots, by the conflux of meeting sap,
Infect the sound pine and divert his grain
Tortive and errant from his course of growth.
Nor, princes, is it matter new to us 10
That we come short of our suppose so far
That after seven years' siege yet Troy walls stand;
Sith every action that hath gone before,
Whereof we have record, trial did draw
Bias and thwart, not answering the aim
And that unbodied figure of the thought
That gave't surmised shape. Why then, you princes,
Do you with cheeks abash'd behold our works,
And call them shames? which are indeed nought else
But the protractive trials of great Jove 20

To find persistive constancy in men:
The fineness of which metal is not found
In fortune's love; for then the bold and coward,
The wise and fool, the artist and unread,
The hard and soft, seem all affined and kin:
But in the wind and tempest of her frown,
Distinction with a broad and powerful fan,
Puffing at all, winnows the light away,
And what hath mass or matter, by itself
Lies rich in virtue and unmingled. 30
Nest. With due observance of thy godlike seat,
Great Agamemnon, Nestor shall apply
Thy latest words. In the reproof of chance
Lies the true proof of men: the sea being smooth,
How many shallow bauble boats dare sail
Upon her patient breast, making their way
With those of nobler bulk!
But let the ruffian Boreas once enrage
The gentle Thetis, and anon behold
The strong-ribb'd bark through liquid mountains cut, 40
Bounding between the two moist elements,
Like Perseus' horse: where's then the saucy boat,
Whose weak untimber'd sides but even now
Co-rivall'd greatness? either to harbour fled,
Or made a toast for Neptune. Even so
Doth valour's show and valour's worth divide
In storms of fortune: for in her ray and brightness
The herd hath more annoyance by the breese
Than by the tiger; but when the splitting wind
Makes flexible the knees of knotted oaks, 50
And flies fled under shade, why then the thing of
courage

As roused with rage with rage doth sympathize,
And with an accent tuned in selfsame key
Retorts to chiding fortune.

Ulyss. Agamemnon,
Thou great commander, nerve and bone of Greece,
Heart of our numbers, soul and only spirit,
In whom the tempers and the minds of all
Should be shut up, hear what Ulysses speaks.
Besides the applause and approbation
The which, [*To Agamemnon*] most mighty for thy
place and sway, 60
[*To Nestor*] And thou most reverend for thy
stretch'd-out life,
I give to both your speeches, which were such
As Agamemnon and the hand of Greece
Should hold up high in brass, and such again
As venerable Nestor, hatch'd in silver,
Should with a bond of air, strong as the axletree
On which heaven rides, knit all the Greekish ears
To his experienced tongue, yet let it please both,
Thou great, and wise, to hear Ulysses speak.

Agam. Speak, Prince of Ithaca; and be't of less
expect 70
That matter needless, of importless burthen,
Divide thy lips, than we are confident,
When rank Thersites opes his mastic jaws,
We shall hear music, wit and oracle.

Ulyss. Troy, yet upon his basis, had been down,
And the great Hector's sword had lack'd a master,
But for these instances.
The specialty of rule hath been neglected:
And, look, how many Grecian tents do stand

Hollow upon this plain, so many hollow factions. 80
When that the general is not like the hive
To whom the foragers shall all repair,
What honey is expected? Degree being vizarded,
The unworthiest shows as fairly in the mask.
The heavens themselves, the planets and this centre,
Observe degree, priority and place,
Insisture, course, proportion, season, form,
Office and custom, in all line of order:
And therefore is the glorious planet Sol
In noble eminence enthroned and sphered 90
Amidst the other; whose medicinable eye
Corrects the ill aspects of planets evil,
And posts like the commandment of a king,
Sans check to good and bad: but when the planets
In evil mixture to disorder wander,
What plagues and what portents, what mutiny,
What raging of the sea, shaking of earth,
Commotion in the winds, frights, changes, horrors,
Divert and crack, rend and deracinate
The unity and married calm of states 100
Quite from their fixture! O, when degree is shaked,
Which is the ladder to all high designs,
The enterprise is sick! How could communities,
Degrees in schools and brotherhoods in cities,
Peaceful commerce from dividable shores,
The primogenitive and due of birth,
Prerogative of age, crowns, sceptres, laurels,
But by degree, stand in authentic place?
Take but degree away, untune that string,
And, hark, what discord follows! each thing meets 110
In mere oppugnancy: the bounded waters

Should lift their bosoms higher than the shores,
And make a sop of all this solid globe:
Strength should be lord of imbecility,
And the rude son should strike his father dead:
Force should be right; or rather, right and wrong,
Between whose endless jar justice resides,
Should lose their names, and so should justice too.
Then every thing includes itself in power,
Power into will, will into appetite; 120
And appetite, an universal wolf,
So doubly seconded with will and power,
Must make perforce an universal prey,
And last eat up himself. Great Agamemnon,
This chaos, when degree is suffocate,
Follows the choking.
And this neglection of degree it is
That by a pace goes backward, with a purpose
It hath to climb. The general's disdain'd
By him one step below; he by the next; 130
That next by him beneath: so every step,
Exampled by the first pace that is sick
Of his superior, grows to an envious fever
Of pale and bloodless emulation:
And 'tis this fever that keeps Troy on foot,
Not her own sinews. To end a tale of length,
Troy in our weakness stands, not in her strength.

Nest. Most wisely hath Ulysses here discover'd
The fever whereof all our power is sick.

Agam. The nature of the sickness found, Ulysses, 140
What is the remedy?

Ulyss. The great Achilles, whom opinion crowns
The sinew and the forehand of our host,

Having his ear full of his airy fame,
Grows dainty of his worth, and in his tent
Lies mocking our designs: with him, Patroclus,
Upon a lazy bed, the livelong day
Breaks scurril jests;
And with ridiculous and awkward action,
Which, slanderer, he imitation calls, 150
He pageants us. Sometime, great Agamemnon,
Thy topless deputation he puts on;
And, like a strutting player, whose conceit
Lies in his hamstring, and doth think it rich
To hear the wooden dialogue and sound
'Twixt his stretch'd footing and the scaffoldage,
Such to-be-pitied and o'er-wrested seeming
He acts thy greatness in: and when he speaks,
'Tis like a chime a-mending; with terms unsquared,
Which, from the tongue of roaring Typhon dropp'd, 160
Would seem hyperboles. At this fusty stuff,
The large Achilles, on his press'd bed lolling,
From his deep chest laughs out a loud applause;
Cries 'Excellent! 'tis Agamemnon just.
Now play me Nestor; hem, and stroke thy beard,
As he being dress'd to some oration.'
That's done; as near as the extremest ends
Of parallels, as like as Vulcan and his wife:
Yet god Achilles still cries 'Excellent!
'Tis Nestor right. Now play him me, Patroclus, 170
Arming to answer in a night alarm.'
And then, forsooth, the faint defects of age
Must be the scene of mirth; to cough and spit,
And, with a palsy fumbling on his gorget,
Shake in and out the rivet: and at this sport

Sir Valour dies; cries 'O, enough, Patroclus;
Or give me ribs of steel! I shall split all
In pleasure of my spleen.' And in this fashion,
All our abilities, gifts, natures, shapes,
Severals and generals of grace exact, 180
Achievements, plots, orders, preventions,
Excitements to the field or speech for truce,
Success or loss, what is or is not, serves
As stuff for these two to make paradoxes.

Nest. And in the imitation of these twain,
Who, as Ulysses says, opinion crowns
With an imperial voice, many are infect.
Ajax is grown self-will'd, and bears his head
In such a rein, in full as proud a place
As broad Achilles; keeps his tent like him; 190
Makes factious feasts; rails on our state of war
Bold as an oracle, and sets Thersites,
A slave whose gall coins slanders like a mint,
To match us in comparisons with dirt,
To weaken and discredit our exposure,
How rank soever rounded in with danger.

Ulyss. They tax our policy and call it cowardice,
Count wisdom as no member of the war,
Forestall prescience, and esteem no act
But that of hand: the still and mental parts 200
That do contrive how many hands shall strike
When fitness calls them on, and know by measure
Of their observant toil the enemies' weight, —
Why, this hath not a finger's dignity:
They call this bed-work, mappery, closet-war;
So that the ram that batters down the wall,
For the great swing and rudeness of his poise,

They place before his hand that made the engine,
Or those that with the fineness of their souls
By reason guide his execution. 210
Nest. Let this be granted, and Achilles' horse
Makes many Thetis' sons. [*Tucket.*
Agam. What trumpet? look, Menelaus.
Men. From Troy.

Enter Æneas

Agam. What would you 'fore our tent?
Æne. Is this great Agamemnon's tent, I pray you?
Agam. Even this.
Æne. May one that is a herald and a prince
Do a fair message to his kingly ears?
Agam. With surety stronger than Achilles' arm 220
'Fore all the Greekish heads, which with one voice
Call Agamemnon head and general.
Æne. Fair leave and large security. How may
A stranger to those most imperial looks
Know them from eyes of other mortals?
Agam. How!
Æne. Ay:
I ask, that I might waken reverence,
And bid the cheek be ready with a blush
Modest as morning when she coldly eyes
The youthful Phœbus: 230
Which is that god in office, guiding men?
Which is the high and mighty Agamemnon?
Agam. This Trojan scorns us; or the men of Troy
Are ceremonious courtiers.
Æne. Courtiers as free, as debonair, unarm'd,
As bending angels; that's their fame in peace:

But when they would seem soldiers, they have galls,
Good arms, strong joints, true swords; and, Jove's
accord,
Nothing so full of heart. But peace, Æneas,
Peace, Trojan; lay thy finger on thy lips! 240
The worthiness of praise distains his worth,
If that the praised himself bring the praise forth:
But what the repining enemy commends,
That breath fame blows; that praise, sole pure,
transcends.

Agam. Sir, you of Troy, call you yourself Æneas?

Æne. Ay, Greek, that is my name.

Agam. What's your affair, I pray you?

Æne. Sir, pardon; 'tis for Agamemnon's ears.

Agam. He hears nought privately that comes
from Troy.

Æne. Nor I from Troy come not to whisper him: 250
I bring a trumpet to awake his ear,
To set his sense on the attentive bent,
And then to speak.

Agam. Speak frankly as the wind;
It is not Agamemnon's sleeping hour:
That thou shalt know, Trojan, he is awake,
He tells thee so himself.

Æne. Trumpet, blow loud,
Send thy brass voice through all these lazy tents;
And every Greek of mettle, let him know,
What Troy means fairly shall be spoke aloud.
[*Trumpet sounds.*
We have, great Agamemnon, here in Troy 260
A prince call'd Hector — Priam is his father —
Who in this dull and long-continued truce

Is rusty grown: he bade me take a trumpet,
And to this purpose speak. Kings, princes, lords!
If there be one among the fair'st of Greece,
That holds his honour higher than his ease,
That seeks his praise more than he fears his peril,
That knows his valour and knows not his fear,
That loves his mistress more than in confession
With truant vows to her own lips he loves, 270
And dare avow her beauty and her worth
In other arms than hers — to him this challenge.
Hector, in view of Trojans and of Greeks,
Shall make it good, or do his best to do it,
He hath a lady, wiser, fairer, truer,
Than ever Greek did compass in his arms;
And will to-morrow with his trumpet call
Midway between your tents and walls of Troy,
To rouse a Grecian that is true in love:
If any come, Hector shall honour him; 280
If none, he'll say in Troy when he retires,
The Grecian dames are sunburnt and not worth
The splinter of a lance. Even so much.

Agam. This shall be told our lovers, Lord Æneas;
If none of them have soul in such a kind,
We left them all at home: but we are soldiers;
And may that soldier a mere recreant prove,
That means not, hath not, or is not in love!
If then one is, or hath, or means to be,
That one meets Hector; if none else, I am he. 290

Nest. Tell him of Nestor, one that was a man
When Hector's grandsire suck'd: he is old now;
But if there be not in our Grecian host
One noble man that hath one spark of fire,

To answer for his love, tell him from me
I'll hide my silver beard in a gold beaver,
And in my vantbrace put this wither'd brawn,
And meeting him will tell him that my lady
Was fairer than his grandam, and as chaste
As may be in the world: his youth in flood, 300
I'll prove this truth with my three drops of blood.

Æne. Now heavens forbid such scarcity of youth!

Ulyss. Amen.

Agam. Fair Lord Æneas, let me touch your hand;
To our pavilion shall I lead you, sir.
Achilles shall have word of this intent;
So shall each lord of Greece, from tent to tent:
Yourself shall feast with us before you go,
And find the welcome of a noble foe.

[*Exeunt all but Ulysses and Nestor.*

Ulyss. Nestor! 310

Nest. What says Ulysses?

Ulyss. I have a young conception in my brain;
Be you my time to bring it to some shape.

Nest. What is 't?

Ulyss. This 'tis:
Blunt wedges rive hard knots: the seeded pride
That hath to this maturity blown up
In rank Achilles must or now be cropp'd,
Or, shedding, breed a nursery of like evil,
To overbulk us all.

Nest. Well, and how? 320

Ulyss. This challenge that the gallant Hector sends,
However it is spread in general name,
Relates in purpose only to Achilles.

Nest. The purpose is perspicuous even as substance,
Whose grossness little characters sum up:
And, in the publication, make no strain,
But that Achilles, were his brain as barren
As banks of Libya, — though, Apollo knows,
'Tis dry enough — will, with great speed of judgement,
Ay, with celerity, find Hector's purpose 330
Pointing on him.

Ulyss. And wake him to the answer, think you?

Nest. Yes, 'tis most meet: who may you else oppose,
That can from Hector bring his honour off,
If not Achilles? Though 't be a sportful combat,
Yet in this trial much opinion dwells;
For here the Trojans taste our dear'st repute
With their finest palate: and trust to me, Ulysses,
Our imputation shall be oddly poised
In this wild action; for the success, 340
Although particular, shall give a scantling
Of good or bad unto the general;
And in such indexes, although small pricks
To their subsequent volumes, there is seen
The baby figure of the giant mass
Of things to come at large. It is supposed
He that meets Hector issues from our choice:
And choice, being mutual act of all our souls,
Makes merit her election, and doth boil,
As 'twere from forth us all, a man distill'd 350
Out of our virtues; who miscarrying,
What heart from hence receives the conquering part,

To steel a strong opinion to themselves?
Which entertain'd, limbs are his instruments,
In no less working than are swords and bows
Directive by the limbs.

Ulyss. Give pardon to my speech;
Therefore 'tis meet Achilles meet not Hector.
Let us, like merchants, show our foulest wares,
And think, perchance, they'll sell; if not, 360
The lustre of the better yet to show,
Shall show the better. Do not consent
That ever Hector and Achilles meet;
For both our honour and our shame in this
Are dogg'd with two strange followers.

Nest. I see them not with my old eyes: what are they?

Ulyss. What glory our Achilles shares from Hector,
Were he not proud, we all should share with him:
But he already is too insolent;
And we were better parch in Afric sun 370
Than in the pride and salt scorn of his eyes,
Should he 'scape Hector fair: if he were foil'd
Why then, we did our main opinion crush
In taint of our best man. No, make a lottery;
And by device let blockish Ajax draw
The sort to fight with Hector: among ourselves
Give him allowance for the better man;
For that will physic the great Myrmidon
Who broils in loud applause, and make him fall
His crest that prouder than blue Iris bends. 380
If the dull brainless Ajax come safe off,
We'll dress him up in voices: if he fail,

Yet go we under our opinion still
That we have better men. But, hit or miss,
Our project's life this shape of sense assumes,
Ajax employ'd plucks down Achilles' plumes.

Nest. Ulysses,
Now I begin to relish thy advice;
And I will give a taste of it forthwith
To Agamemnon: go we to him straight. 390
Two curs shall tame each other: pride alone
Must tarre the mastiffs on, as 'twere their bone.
[*Exeunt.*

ACT II

Scene I — *The Grecian Camp*

Enter Ajax *and* Thersites

Ajax. Thersites!

Ther. Agamemnon — how if he had boils — full, all over, generally?

Ajax. Thersites!

Ther. And those boils did run? — Say so, — did not the general run then? were not that a botchy core?

Ajax. Dog!

Ther. Then would come some matter from him; I see none now. 10

Ajax. Thou bitch-wolf's son, canst thou not hear? Feel, then. [*Strikes him.*

Ther. The plague of Greece upon thee, thou mongrel beef-witted lord!

Ajax. Speak then, thou vinewed'st leaven, speak: I will beat thee into handsomeness.

Ther. I shall sooner rail thee into wit and holiness: but, I think, thy horse will sooner con an oration than thou learn a prayer without book. Thou canst strike, canst thou? a red murrain o' thy jade's tricks! 20

Ajax. Toadstool, learn me the proclamation.

Ther. Dost thou think I have no sense, thou strikest me thus?

Ajax. The proclamation!

Ther. Thou art proclaimed a fool, I think.

Ajax. Do not, porpentine, do not; my fingers itch.

Ther. I would thou didst itch from head to foot, and I had the scratching of thee; I would make 30 thee the loathsomest scab in Greece. When thou art forth in the incursions, thou strikest as slow as another.

Ajax. I say, the proclamation!

Ther. Thou grumblest and railest every hour on Achilles, and thou art as full of envy at his greatness as Cerberus is at Proserpina's beauty, ay, that thou barkest at him.

Ajax. Mistress Thersites!

Ther. Thou shouldst strike him. 40

Ajax. Cobloaf!

Ther. He would pun thee into shivers with his fist, as a sailor breaks a biscuit.

Ajax. [*Beating him*] You whoreson cur!

Ther. Do, do.

Ajax. Thou stool for a witch!

Ther. Ay, do, do; thou sodden-witted lord! thou hast no more brain than I have in mine elbows;

an assinego may tutor thee: thou scurvy-valiant ass! thou art here but to thrash Trojans; and 50
thou art bought and sold among those of any wit, like a barbarian slave. If thou use to beat me, I will begin at thy heel and tell what thou art by inches, thou thing of no bowels, thou!

Ajax. You dog!

Ther. You scurvy lord!

Ajax. [*Beating him*] You cur!

Ther. Mars his idiot! do, rudeness; do, camel, do, do.

Enter Achilles *and* Patroclus

Achil. Why, how now, Ajax! wherefore do ye 60
thus? How now, Thersites! what's the matter, man?

Ther. You see him there, do you?

Achil. Ay; what's the matter?

Ther. Nay, look upon him.

Achil. So I do: what's the matter?

Ther. Nay, but regard him well.

Achil. 'Well!' why, so I do.

Ther. But yet you look not well upon him; for, whosoever you take him to be, he is Ajax. 70

Achil. I know that, fool.

Ther. Ay, but that fool knows not himself.

Ajax. Therefore I beat thee.

Ther. Lo, lo, lo, lo, what modicums of wit he utters! his evasions have ears thus long. I have bobbed his brain more than he has beat my bones: I will buy nine sparrows for a penny, and his pia mater is not worth the ninth part of a sparrow.

This lord, Achilles, Ajax, who wears his wit in his belly and his guts in his head, I'll tell you what 80 I say of him.

Achil. What?

Ther. I say, this Ajax — [*Ajax offers to strike him.*

Achil. Nay, good Ajax.

Ther. Has not so much wit —

Achil. Nay, I must hold you.

Ther. As will stop the eye of Helen's needle, for whom he comes to fight.

Achil. Peace, fool!

Ther. I would have peace and quietness, but 90 the fool will not: he there: that he: look you there!

Ajax. O thou damned cur! I shall —

Achil. Will you set your wit to a fool's?

Ther. No, I warrant you; for a fool's will shame it.

Patr. Good words, Thersites.

Achil. What's the quarrel?

Ajax. I bade the vile owl go learn me the tenour of the proclamation, and he rails upon me. 100

Ther. I serve thee not.

Ajax. Well, go to, go to.

Ther. I serve here voluntary.

Achil. Your last service was sufferance, 'twas not voluntary; no man is beaten voluntary: Ajax was here the voluntary, and you as under an impress.

Ther. E'en so; a great deal of your wit too lies in your sinews, or else there be liars. Hector shall have a great catch, if he knock out either 110 of your brains: a' were as good crack a fusty nut with no kernel.

Achil. What, with me too, Thersites?

Ther. There's Ulysses and old Nestor, whose wit was mouldy ere your grandsires had nails on their toes, yoke you like draught-oxen, and make you plough up the wars.

Achil. What? what?

Ther. Yes, good sooth: to, Achilles! to, Ajax! to! 120

Ajax. I shall cut out your tongue.

Ther. 'Tis no matter; I shall speak as much as thou afterwards.

Patr. No more words, Thersites; peace!

Ther. I will hold my peace when Achilles' brooch bids me, shall I?

Achil. There's for you, Patroclus.

Ther. I will see you hanged, like clotpoles, ere I come any more to your tents: I will keep where there is wit stirring, and leave the faction of fools. 130 [*Exit.*

Patr. A good riddance.

Achil. Marry, this, sir, is proclaim'd through all our host:
That Hector, by the fifth hour of the sun,
Will with a trumpet 'twixt our tents and Troy
To-morrow morning call some knight to arms
That hath a stomach, and such a one that dare
Maintain — I know not what: 'tis trash. Farewell.

Ajax. Farewell. Who shall answer him?

Achil. I know not; 'tis put to lottery; otherwise 140

He knew his man.

Ajax. O, meaning you. I will go learn more of it.
[*Exeunt.*

SCENE II — *Troy. A room in Priam's palace*

Enter PRIAM, HECTOR, TROILUS, PARIS, *and* HELENUS

Pri. After so many hours, lives, speeches spent,
Thus once again says Nestor from the Greeks:
'Deliver Helen, and all damage else,
As honour, loss of time, travail, expense,
Wounds, friends, and what else dear that is consumed
In hot digestion of this cormorant war,
Shall be struck off.' Hector, what say you to 't?

Hect. Though no man lesser fears the Greeks than I
As far as toucheth my particular,
Yet, dread Priam, 10
There is no lady of more softer bowels,
More spongy to suck in the sense of fear,
More ready to cry out 'Who knows what follows?'
Than Hector is: the wound of peace is surety,
Surety secure: but modest doubt is call'd
The beacon of the wise, the tent that searches
To the bottom of the worst. Let Helen go.
Since the first sword was drawn about this question,
Every tithe soul, 'mongst many thousand dismes,
Hath been as dear as Helen; I mean, of ours: 20
If we have lost so many tenths of ours,
To guard a thing not ours, nor worth to us,
Had it our name, the value of one ten,
What merit's in that reason which denies
The yielding of her up?

Tro. Fie, fie, my brother!
Weigh you the worth and honour of a king,
So great as our dread father, in a scale
Of common ounces? will you with counters sum
The past proportion of his infinite?
And buckle in a waist most fathomless 30
With spans and inches so diminutive
As fears and reasons? fie, for godly shame!

Hel. No marvel, though you bite so sharp at reasons,
You are so empty of them. Should not our father
Bear the great sway of his affairs with reasons,
Because your speech hath none that tells him so?

Tro. You are for dreams and slumbers, brother priest;
You fur your gloves with reason. Here are your reasons:
You know an enemy intends you harm;
You know a sword employ'd is perilous, 40
And reason flies the object of all harm:
Who marvels then, when Helenus beholds
A Grecian and his sword, if he do set
The very wings of reason to his heels,
And fly like chidden Mercury from Jove,
Or like a star disorb'd? Nay, if we talk of reason,
Let's shut our gates, and sleep: manhood and honour
Should have hare hearts, would they but fat their thoughts
With this cramm'd reason: reason and respect
Make livers pale and lustihood deject. 50

Hect. Brother, she is not worth what she doth cost
The holding.

Tro. What's aught, but as 'tis valued?
Hect. But value dwells not in particular will;
It holds his estimate and dignity
As well wherein 'tis precious of itself
As in the prizer: 'tis mad idolatry
To make the service greater than the god;
And the will dotes, that is attributive
To what infectiously itself affects,
Without some image of the affected merit. 60
Tro. I take to-day a wife, and my election
Is led on in the conduct of my will;
My will enkindled by mine eyes and ears,
Two traded pilots 'twixt the dangerous shores
Of will and judgement: how may I avoid,
Although my will distaste what it elected,
The wife I chose? there can be no evasion
To blench from this, and to stand firm by honour.
We turn not back the silks upon the merchant
When we have soil'd them, nor the remainder viands 70
We do not throw in unrespective sieve,
Because we now are full. It was thought meet
Paris should do some vengeance on the Greeks:
Your breath of full consent bellied his sails;
The seas and winds, old wranglers, took a truce,
And did him service: he touch'd the ports desired;
And for an old aunt whom the Greeks held captive
He brought a Grecian queen, whose youth and
freshness
Wrinkles Apollo's and makes stale the morning.
Why keep we her? the Grecians keep our aunt: 80
Is she worth keeping? why, she is a pearl,
Whose price hath launch'd above a thousand ships,

And turn'd crown'd kings to merchants.
If you'll avouch 'twas wisdom Paris went,
As you must needs, for you all cried 'Go, go,'
If you'll confess he brought home noble prize,
As you must needs, for you all clapp'd your hands,
And cried 'Inestimable!' why do you now
The issue of your proper wisdoms rate,
And do a deed that Fortune never did, 90
Beggar the estimation which you prized
Richer than sea and land? O, theft most base,
That we have stol'n what we do fear to keep!
But thieves unworthy of a thing so stol'n,
That in their country did them that disgrace,
We fear to warrant in our native place!

Cas. [*Within*] Cry, Trojans, cry!

Pri. What noise? what shriek is this?

Tro. 'Tis our mad sister, I do know her voice.

Cas. [*Within*] Cry, Trojans!

Hect. It is Cassandra. 100

Enter CASSANDRA, *raving, with her hair about her ears*

Cas. Cry, Trojans, cry! lend me ten thousand eyes,
And I will fill them with prophetic tears.

Hect. Peace, sister, peace!

Cas. Virgins and boys, mid age and wrinkled eld,
Soft infancy, that nothing canst but cry,
Add to my clamours! let us pay betimes
A moiety of that mass of moan to come.
Cry, Trojans, cry! practise your eyes with tears!
Troy must not be, nor goodly Ilion stand;
Our firebrand brother, Paris, burns us all. 110

Cry, Trojan, cry! a Helen and a woe:
Cry, cry! Troy burns, or else let Helen go. [*Exit.*

Hect. Now, youthful Troilus, do not these high strains
Of divination in our sister work
Some touches of remorse? or is your blood
So madly hot that no discourse of reason,
Nor fear of bad success in a bad cause,
Can qualify the same?

Tro. Why, brother Hector,
We may not think the justness of each act
Such and no other than event doth form it; 120
Nor once deject the courage of our minds,
Because Cassandra's mad: her brain-sick raptures
Cannot distaste the goodness of a quarrel
Which hath our several honours all engaged
To make it gracious. For my private part,
I am no more touch'd than all Priam's sons:
And Jove forbid there should be done amongst us
Such things as might offend the weakest spleen
To fight for and maintain!

Par. Else might the world convince of levity 130
As well my undertakings as your counsels:
But I attest the gods, your full consent
Gave wings to my propension, and cut off
All fears attending on so dire a project.
For what, alas, can these my single arms?
What propugnation is in one man's valour,
To stand the push and enmity of those
This quarrel would excite? Yet, I protest,
Were I alone to pass the difficulties,
And had as ample power as I have will, 140

Paris should ne'er retract what he hath done,
Nor faint in the pursuit.
Pri. Paris, you speak
Like one besotted on your sweet delights:
You have the honey still, but these the gall;
So to be valiant is no praise at all.
Par. Sir, I propose not merely to myself
The pleasures such a beauty brings with it;
But I would have the soil of her fair rape
Wiped off in honourable keeping her.
What treason were it to the ransack'd queen, 150
Disgrace to your great worths, and shame to me,
Now to deliver her possession up
On terms of base compulsion! Can it be
That so degenerate a strain as this
Should once set footing in your generous bosoms?
There's not the meanest spirit on our party,
Without a heart to dare, or sword to draw,
When Helen is defended, nor none so noble,
Whose life were ill bestow'd, or death unfamed,
Where Helen is the subject: then, I say, 160
Well may we fight for her, whom, we know well,
The world's large spaces cannot parallel.
Hect. Paris and Troilus, you have both said well;
And on the cause and question now in hand
Have glozed, but superficially; not much
Unlike young men, whom Aristotle thought
Unfit to hear moral philosophy.
The reasons you allege do more conduce
To the hot passion of distemper'd blood,
Than to make up a free determination 170
'Twixt right and wrong; for pleasure and revenge

Have ears more deaf than adders to the voice
Of any true decision. Nature craves
All dues be render'd to their owners: now,
What nearer debt in all humanity
Than wife is to the husband? If this law
Of nature be corrupted through affection,
And that great minds, of partial indulgence
To their benumbed wills, resist the same,
There is a law in each well-order'd nation 180
To curb those raging appetites that are
Most disobedient and refractory.
If Helen then be wife to Sparta's king,
As it is known she is, these moral laws
Of nature and of nations speak aloud
To have her back return'd: thus to persist
In doing wrong extenuates not wrong,
But makes it much more heavy. Hector's opinion
Is this in way of truth: yet, ne'ertheless,
My spritely brethren, I propend to you 190
In resolution to keep Helen still;
For 'tis a cause that hath no mean dependance
Upon our joint and several dignities.

Tro. Why, there you touch'd the life of our design:
Were it not glory that we more affected
Than the performance of our heaving spleens,
I would not wish a drop of Trojan blood
Spent more in her defence. But, worthy Hector,
She is a theme of honour and renown;
A spur to valiant and magnanimous deeds, 200
Whose present courage may beat down our foes,
And fame in time to come canonize us:

For, I presume, brave Hector would not lose
So rich advantage of a promised glory
As smiles upon the forehead of this action
For the wide world's revenue.

Hect. I am yours,
You valiant offspring of great Priamus.
I have a roisting challenge sent amongst
The dull and factious nobles of the Greeks,
Will strike amazement to their drowsy spirits: 210
I was advertised their great general slept,
Whilst emulation in the army crept:
This, I presume, will wake him. [*Exeunt.*

SCENE III — *The Grecian camp. Before the tent of Achilles*

Enter THERSITES, *solus*

Ther. How now, Thersites! what, lost in the labyrinth of thy fury! Shall the elephant Ajax carry it thus? he beats me, and I rail at him: O, worthy satisfaction! would it were otherwise; that I could beat him, whilst he railed at me. 'Sfoot, I'll learn to conjure and raise devils, but I'll see some issue of my spiteful execrations. Then there's Achilles, a rare enginer. If Troy be not taken till these two undermine it, the walls will stand till they fall of themselves. O thou great thunder- 10 darter of Olympus, forget that thou art Jove, the king of gods, and, Mercury, lose all the serpentine craft of thy caduceus, if ye take not that little little less than little wit from them that they have! which short-armed ignorance itself knows is so abundant scarce, it will not in circumvention deliver a fly from a spider, without drawing their massy irons and cutting the web. After this, the vengeance on the whole camp! or, rather, the Neapolitan bone-ache! for that, methinks, 20 is the curse dependant on those that war for a placket. I have said my prayers; and devil Envy say amen. What, ho! my Lord Achilles!

Enter PATROCLUS

Patr. Who's there? Thersites! Good Thersites, come in and rail.

Ther. If I could ha' remembered a gilt counterfeit, thou wouldst not have slipped out of my contemplation: but it is no matter; thyself upon thyself! The common curse of mankind, folly and ignorance, be thine in great revenue! heaven bless 30 thee from a tutor, and discipline come not near thee! Let thy blood be thy direction till thy death! then if she that lays thee out says thou art a fair corse, I'll be sworn and sworn upon 't she never shrouded any but lazars. Amen. Where's Achilles?

Patr. What, art thou devout? wast thou in prayer?

Ther. Ay; the heavens hear me!

Patr. Amen.

Enter ACHILLES

Achil. Who's there? 40

Patr. Thersites, my lord.

Achil. Where, where? Art thou come? why, my cheese, my digestion, why hast thou not served thyself in to my table so many meals? Come, what's Agamemnon?

Ther. Thy commander, Achilles: then tell me, Patroclus, what's Achilles?

Patr. Thy lord, Thersites: then tell me, I pray thee, what's thyself?

Ther. Thy knower, Patroclus: then tell me, Patroclus, what art thou? 50

Patr. Thou mayst tell that knowest.

Achil. O, tell, tell.

Ther. I'll decline the whole question. Agamemnon commands Achilles; Achilles is my lord; I am Patroclus' knower, and Patroclus is a fool.

Patr. You rascal!

Ther. Peace, fool! I have not done.

Achil. He is a privileged man. Proceed, Thersites. 60

Ther. Agamemnon is a fool; Achilles is a fool; Thersites is a fool, and, as aforesaid, Patroclus is a fool.

Achil. Derive this; come.

Ther. Agamemnon is a fool to offer to command Achilles; Achilles is a fool to be commanded of Agamemnon; Thersites is a fool to serve such a fool; and Patroclus is a fool positive.

Patr. Why am I a fool?

Ther. Make that demand of the prover. It suffices me thou art. Look you, who comes here? 70

Achil. Patroclus, I'll speak with nobody. Come in with me, Thersites. [*Exit.*

Ther. Here is such patchery, such juggling and such knavery! all the argument is a cuckold and a whore; a good quarrel to draw emulous factions and bleed to death upon. Now, the dry serpigo on the subject! and war and lechery confound all! [*Exit.*

Enter AGAMEMNON, ULYSSES, NESTOR, DIOMEDES, *and* AJAX

Agam. Where is Achilles? 80
Patr. Within his tent; but ill-disposed, my lord.
Agam. Let it be known to him that we are here.
He shent our messengers; and we lay by
Our appertainments, visiting of him:
Let him be told so, lest perchance he think
We dare not move the question of our place,
Or know not what we are.
Patr. I shall say so to him. [*Exit.*
Ulyss. We saw him at the opening of his tent:
He is not sick.

Ajax. Yes, lion-sick, sick of proud heart: you 90 may call it melancholy, if you will favour the man; but, by my head, 'tis pride: but why, why? let him show us the cause. A word, my lord. [*Takes Agamemnon aside.*

Nest. What moves Ajax thus to bay at him?

Ulyss. Achilles hath inveigled his fool from him.

Nest. Who, Thersites?

Ulyss. He.

Nest. Then will Ajax lack matter, if he have 100 lost his argument.

Ulyss. No, you see, he is his argument that has his argument, Achilles.

Nest. All the better; their fraction is more our

wish than their faction: but it was a strong composure a fool could disunite.

Ulyss. The amity that wisdom knits not, folly may easily untie.

Re-enter Patroclus

Here comes Patroclus.

Nest. No Achilles with him. 110

Ulyss. The elephant hath joints, but none for courtesy: his legs are legs for necessity, not for flexure.

Patr. Achilles bids me say, he is much sorry,
If anything more than your sport and pleasure
Did move your greatness and this noble state
To call upon him; he hopes it is no other
But for your health and your digestion sake,
An after-dinner's breath.

Agam. Hear you, Patroclus:
We are too well acquainted with these answers: 120
But his evasion, wing'd thus swift with scorn,
Cannot outfly our apprehensions.
Much attribute he hath, and much the reason
Why we ascribe it to him: yet all his virtues,
Not virtuously on his own part beheld,
Do in our eyes begin to lose their gloss,
Yea, like fair fruit in an unwholesome dish,
Are like to rot untasted. Go and tell him,
We come to speak with him; and you shall not sin,
If you do say we think him over-proud 130
And under-honest; in self-assumption greater
Than in the note of judgement; and worthier than himself

Here tend the savage strangeness he puts on,
Disguise the holy strength of their command,
And underwrite in an observing kind
His humorous predominance; yea, watch
His pettish lunes, his ebbs, his flows, as if
The passage and whole carriage of this action
Rode on his tide. Go tell him this, and add,
That if he overhold his price so much, 140
We'll none of him, but let him, like an engine
Not portable, lie under this report:
'Bring action hither, this cannot go to war:
A stirring dwarf we do allowance give
Before a sleeping giant:' tell him so.

Patr. I shall; and bring his answer presently.
[*Exit.*

Agam. In second voice we'll not be satisfied;
We come to speak with him. Ulysses, enter you.
[*Exit Ulysses.*

Ajax. What is he more than another?

Agam. No more than what he thinks he is. 150

Ajax. Is he so much? Do you not think he thinks himself a better man than I am?

Agam. No question.

Ajax. Will you subscribe his thought and say he is?

Agam. No, noble Ajax; you are as strong, as valiant, as wise, no less noble, much more gentle and altogether more tractable.

Ajax. Why should a man be proud? How doth pride grow? I know not what pride is. 160

Agam. Your mind is the clearer, Ajax, and your virtues the fairer. He that is proud eats up himself: pride is his own glass, his own trumpet, his own chronicle; and whatever praises itself but in the deed, devours the deed in the praise.

Ajax. I do hate a proud man, as I hate the engendering of toads.

Nest. [*Aside*] Yet he loves himself: is 't not strange?

Re-enter ULYSSES

Ulyss. Achilles will not to the field to-morrow. 170

Agam. What's his excuse?

Ulyss. He doth rely on none,
But carries on the stream of his dispose,
Without observance or respect of any,
In will peculiar and in self-admission.

Agam. Why will he not, upon our fair request,
Untent his person, and share the air with us?

Ulyss. Things small as nothing, for request's sake only
He makes important: possess'd he is with greatness,
And speaks not to himself but with a pride
That quarrels at self-breath: imagined worth 180
Holds in his blood such swol'n and hot discourse
That 'twixt his mental and his active parts
Kingdom'd Achilles in commotion rages
And batters down himself: what should I say?
He is so plaguy proud that the death-tokens of it
Cry 'No recovery.'

Agam. Let Ajax go to him.
Dear lord, go you and greet him in his tent:
'Tis said he holds you well, and will be led
At your request a little from himself.

Ulyss. O Agamemnon, let it not be so! 190
We'll consecrate the steps that Ajax makes
When they go from Achilles. Shall the proud lord
That bastes his arrogance with his own seam,
And never suffers matter of the world
Enter his thoughts, save such as do revolve
And ruminate himself, shall he be worshipp'd
Of that we hold an idol more than he?
No, this thrice worthy and right valiant lord
Must not so stale his palm, nobly acquired,
Nor, by my will, assubjugate his merit, 200
As amply titled as Achilles is,
By going to Achilles:
That were to enlard his fat-already pride,
And add more coals to Cancer when he burns
With entertaining great Hyperion.
This lord go to him! Jupiter forbid,
And say in thunder 'Achilles go to him.'

Nest. [*Aside*] O, this is well; he rubs the vein of him.

Dio. [*Aside*] And how his silence drinks up 210 this applause!

Ajax. If I go to him, with my armed fist
I'll pash him o'er the face.

Agam. O, no, you shall not go.

Ajax. An a' be proud with me, I'll pheeze his pride:
Let me go to him.

Ulyss. Not for the worth that hangs upon our quarrel.

Ajax. A paltry, insolent fellow!

Nest. [*Aside*] How he describes himself! 220

Ajax. Can he not be sociable?

Ulyss. [*Aside*] The raven chides blackness.

Ajax. I'll let his humours blood.

Agam. [*Aside*] He will be the physician that should be the patient.

Ajax. An all men were o' my mind, —

Ulyss. [*Aside*] Wit would be out of fashion.

Ajax. A' should not bear it so, a' should eat swords first: shall pride carry it?

Nest. [*Aside*] An 'twould, you'd carry half. 230

Ulyss. [*Aside*] A' would have ten shares.

Ajax. I will knead him, I'll make him supple.

Nest. [*Aside*] He's not yet through warm: force him with praises: pour in, pour in; his ambition is dry.

Ulyss. [*To Agamemnon*] My lord, you feed
too much on this dislike.

Nest. Our noble general, do not do so.

Dio. You must prepare to fight without Achilles.

Ulyss. Why, 'tis this naming of him does him
harm.
Here is a man — but 'tis before his face; 240
I will be silent.

Nest. Wherefore should you so?
He is not emulous, as Achilles is.

Ulyss. Know the whole world, he is as valiant.

Ajax. A whoreson dog, that shall palter thus with us! Would he were a Trojan!

Nest. What a vice were it in Ajax now —

Ulyss. If he were proud, —

Dio. Or covetous of praise, —

Ulyss. Ay, or surly borne, —

Dio. Or strange, or self-affected! 250

Ulyss. Thank the heavens, lord, thou art of sweet composure;
Praise him that got thee, she that gave thee suck:
Famed be thy tutor, and thy parts of nature
Thrice-famed, beyond all erudition:
But he that disciplined thine arms to fight,
Let Mars divide eternity in twain,
And give him half: and, for thy vigour,
Bull-bearing Milo his addition yield
To sinewy Ajax. I will not praise thy wisdom,
Which, like a bourn, a pale, a shore, confines 260
Thy spacious and dilated parts: here's Nestor,
Instructed by the antiquary times,
He must, he is, he cannot but be wise;
But pardon, father Nestor, were your days
As green as Ajax', and your brain so temper'd,
You should not have the eminence of him,
But be as Ajax.

Ajax. Shall I call you father?

Nest. Ay, my good son.

Dio. Be ruled by him, Lord Ajax.

Ulyss. There is no tarrying here; the hart Achilles
Keeps thicket. Please it our great general 270
To call together all his state of war:
Fresh kings are come to Troy: to-morrow
We must with all our main of power stand fast:
And here's a lord, come knights from east to west,
And cull their flower, Ajax shall cope the best.

Agam. Go we to council. Let Achilles sleep:
Light boats sail swift, though greater hulks draw deep. [*Exeunt.*

ACT III

Scene I — *Troy. A room in Priam's palace*

Enter Pandarus *and a* Servant

Pan. Friend, you, pray you, a word: do you not follow the young Lord Paris?

Serv. Ay, sir, when he goes before me.

Pan. You depend upon him, I mean?

Serv. Sir, I do depend upon the Lord.

Pan. You depend upon a noble gentleman; I must needs praise him.

Serv. The Lord be praised!

Pan. You know me, do you not?

Serv. Faith, sir, superficially. 10

Pan. Friend, know me better; I am the Lord Pandarus.

Serv. I hope I shall know your honour better.

Pan. I do desire it.

Serv. You are in the state of grace.

Pan. Grace! not so, friend; honour and lordship are my titles. [*Music within.*] What music is this?

Serv. I do but partly know, sir: it is music in parts. 20

Pan. Know you the musicians?

Serv. Wholly, sir.

Pan. Who play they to?

Serv. To the hearers, sir.

Pan. At whose pleasure, friend?

Serv. At mine, sir, and theirs that love music.

Pan. Command, I mean, friend.

Serv. Who shall I command, sir?

Pan. Friend, we understand not one another: I am too courtly, and thou art too cunning. At 30 whose request do these men play?

Serv. That's to 't, indeed, sir: marry, sir, at the request of Paris my lord, who is there in person; with him, the mortal Venus, the heart-blood of beauty, love's invisible soul.

Pan. Who, my cousin Cressida?

Serv. No, sir, Helen: could not you find out that by her attributes?

Pan. It should seem, fellow, that thou hast not seen the Lady Cressida. I come to speak with 40 Paris from the Prince Troilus: I will make a complimental assault upon him, for my business seethes.

Serv. Sodden business! there's a stewed phrase indeed!

Enter PARIS *and* HELEN, *attended*

Pan. Fair be to you, my lord, and to all this fair company! fair desires, in all fair measure, fairly guide them! especially to you, fair queen! fair thoughts be your fair pillow!

Helen. Dear lord, you are full of fair words. 50

Pan. You speak your fair pleasure, sweet queen. Fair prince, here is good broken music.

Par. You have broke it, cousin: and, by my life, you shall make it whole again; you shall piece it out with a piece of your performance. Nell, he is full of harmony.

Pan. Truly, lady, no.

Helen. O, sir, —

Pan. Rude, in sooth; in good sooth, very rude.

Par. Well said, my lord! well, you say so in fits. 60

Pan. I have business to my lord, dear queen. My lord, will you vouchsafe me a word?

Helen. Nay, this shall not hedge us out: we'll hear you sing, certainly.

Pan. Well, sweet queen, you are pleasant with me. But, marry, thus, my lord: my dear lord, and most esteemed friend, your brother Troilus —

Helen. My Lord Pandarus; honey-sweet lord, —

Pan. Go to, sweet queen, go to: — commends 70 himself most affectionately to you —

Helen. You shall not bob us out of our melody: if you do, our melancholy upon your head!

Pan. Sweet queen, sweet queen; that's a sweet queen, i' faith.

Helen. And to make a sweet lady sad is a sour offence.

Pan. Nay, that shall not serve your turn; that shall it not, in truth, la. Nay, I care not for such words; no, no. And, my lord, he desires 80 you, that if the king call for him at supper, you will make his excuse.

Helen. My Lord Pandarus, —

Pan. What says my sweet queen, my very very sweet queen?

Par. What exploit's in hand? where sups he to-night?

Helen. Nay, but, my lord, —

Pan. What says my sweet queen! My cousin

will fall out with you. You must not know where 90
he sups.

Par. I'll lay my life, with my disposer Cressida.

Pan. No, no, no such matter; you are wide: come, your disposer is sick.

Par. Well, I'll make excuse.

Pan. Ay, good my lord. Why should you say Cressida? no, your poor disposer's sick.

Par. I spy.

Pan. You spy! what do you spy? Come, give 100
me an instrument. Now, sweet queen.

Helen. Why, this is kindly done.

Pan. My niece is horribly in love with a thing you have, sweet queen.

Helen. She shall have it, my lord, if it be not my lord Paris.

Pan. He! no, she'll none of him; they two are twain.

Helen. Falling in, after falling out, may make
them three. 110

Pan. Come, come, I'll hear no more of this; I'll sing you a song now.

Helen. Ay, ay, prithee now. By my troth, sweet lord, thou hast a fine forehead.

Pan. Ay, you may, you may.

Helen. Let thy song be love: this love will undo us all. O Cupid, Cupid, Cupid!

Pan. Love! ay, that it shall, i' faith.

Par. Ay, good now, love, love, nothing but
love. 120

Pan. In good troth, it begins so. [*Sings.*

Love, love, nothing but love, still more!
For, O, love's bow
Shoots buck and doe:
The shaft confounds,
Not that it wounds,
But tickles still the sore.
These lovers cry Oh! oh! they die:
Ye that which seems the wound to kill,
Doth turn oh! oh! to ha! ha! he! 130
So dying love lives still:
Oh! oh! a while, but ha! ha! ha!
Oh! oh! groans out for ha! ha! ha!
Heigh-ho!

Helen. In love, i' faith, to the very tip of the nose.

Par. He eats nothing but doves, love, and that breeds hot blood, and hot blood begets hot thoughts, and hot thoughts beget hot deeds, and hot deeds is love. 140

Pan. Is this the generation of love? hot blood, hot thoughts and hot deeds? Why, they are vipers: is love a generation of vipers? Sweet lord, who's afield to-day?

Par. Hector, Deiphobus, Helenus, Antenor, and all the gallantry of Troy: I would fain have armed to-day, but my Nell would not have it so. How chance my brother Troilus went not?

Helen. He hangs the lip at something: you know all, Lord Pandarus. 150

Pan. Not I, honey-sweet queen. I long to hear how they sped to-day. You'll remember your brother's excuse?

Par. To a hair.

Pan. Farewell, sweet queen.

Helen. Commend me to your niece.

Pan. I will, sweet queen. [*Exit.*

[*A retreat sounded.*

Par. They're come from field: let us to Priam's hall,
To greet the warriors. Sweet Helen, I must woo you
To help unarm our Hector: his stubborn buckles, 160
With these your white enchanting fingers touch'd,
Shall more obey than to the edge of steel
Or force of Greekish sinews; you shall do more
Than all the island kings, — disarm great Hector.

Helen. 'Twill make us proud to be his servant, Paris;
Yes, what he shall receive of us in duty
Gives us more palm in beauty than we have,
Yea, overshines ourself.

Par. Sweet, above thought I love thee. [*Exeunt.*

SCENE II — *An orchard to Pandarus' house*

Enter PANDARUS *and* TROILUS' BOY, *meeting*

Pan. How now! where's thy master? at my cousin Cressida's?

Boy. No, sir; he stays for you to conduct him thither.

Pan. O, here he comes.

Enter TROILUS

How now, how now!

Tro. Sirrah, walk off. [*Exit Boy.*

Pan. Have you seen my cousin?

Tro. No, Pandarus: I stalk about her door,
Like a strange soul upon the Stygian banks 10
Staying for waftage. O, be thou my Charon,
And give me swift transportance to those fields
Where I may wallow in the lily-beds
Proposed for the deserver! O gentle Pandarus,
From Cupid's shoulder pluck his painted wings,
And fly with me to Cressid!

Pan. Walk here i' the orchard, I'll bring her straight. [*Exit.*

Tro. I am giddy; expectation whirls me round.
The imaginary relish is so sweet
That it enchants my sense: what will it be, 20
When that the watery palates taste indeed
Love's thrice repured nectar? death, I fear me,
Swounding destruction, or some joy too fine,
Too subtle-potent, tuned too sharp in sweetness,
For the capacity of my ruder powers:
I fear it much, and I do fear besides
That I shall lose distinction in my joys,
As doth a battle, when they charge on heaps
The enemy flying.

Re-enter PANDARUS

Pan. She's making her ready, she'll come straight: 30
you must be witty now. She does so blush, and
fetches her wind so short, as if she were frayed
with a sprite: I'll fetch her. It is the prettiest
villain: she fetches her breath as short as a new-
ta'en sparrow. [*Exit.*

Tro. Even such a passion doth embrace my bosom:

My heart beats thicker than a feverous pulse;
And all my powers do their bestowing lose,
Like vassalage at unawares encountering
The eye of majesty. 40

Re-enter PANDARUS *with* CRESSIDA

Pan. Come, come, what need you blush? shame's a baby. Here she is now: swear the oaths now to her that you have sworn to me. What, are you gone again? you must be watched ere you be made tame, must you? Come your ways, come your ways; an you draw backward, we'll put you i' the fills. Why do you not speak to her? Come, draw this curtain, and let's see your picture. Alas the day, how loath you are to offend daylight! an 'twere dark, you'd close sooner. 50 So, so; rub on, and kiss the mistress. How now! a kiss in fee-farm! build there, carpenter; the air is sweet. Nay, you shall fight your hearts out ere I part you. The falcon as the tercel, for all the ducks i' the river: go to, go to.

Tro. You have bereft me of all words, lady.

Pan. Words pay no debts, give her deeds: but she'll bereave you o' the deeds too, if she call your activity in question. What, billing again? Here's 'In witness whereof the parties inter- 60 changeably' — Come in, come in: I'll go get a fire. [*Exit.*

Cres. Will you walk in, my lord?

Tro. O Cressida, how often have I wished me thus!

Cres. Wished, my lord? — The gods grant — O my lord!

Tro. What should they grant? what makes this pretty abruption? What too curious dreg espies my sweet lady in the fountain of our love? 70

Cres. More dregs than water, if my fears have eyes.

Tro. Fears make devils of cherubins; they never see truly.

Cres. Blind fear, that seeing reason leads, finds safer footing than blind reason stumbling without fear: to fear the worst oft cures the worse.

Tro. O, let my lady apprehend no fear: in all Cupid's pageant there is presented no monster. 80

Cres. Nor nothing monstrous neither?

Tro. Nothing, but our undertakings; when we vow to weep seas, live in fire, eat rocks, tame tigers; thinking it harder for our mistress to devise imposition enough than for us to undergo any difficulty imposed. This is the monstruosity in love, lady, that the will is infinite and the execution confined, that the desire is boundless and the act a slave to limit.

Cres. They say, all lovers swear more per- 90 formance than they are able, and yet reserve an ability that they never perform, vowing more than the perfection of ten, and discharging less than the tenth part of one. They that have the voice of lions and the act of hares, are they not monsters?

Tro. Are there such? such are not we: praise us as we are tasted, allow us as we prove; our head shall go bare till merit crown it: no perfection in reversion shall have a praise in present: we will not name desert before his birth, and, 100 being born, his addition shall be humble. Few words to fair faith: Troilus shall be such to Cressid as what envy can say worst shall be a mock for his truth, and what truth can speak truest, not truer than Troilus.

Cres. Will you walk in, my lord?

Re-enter PANDARUS

Pan. What, blushing still? have you not done talking yet?

Cres. Well, uncle, what folly I commit, I dedicate to you. 110

Pan. I thank you for that: if my lord get a boy of you, you'll give him me. Be true to my lord: if he flinch, chide me for it.

Tro. You know now your hostages; your uncle's word and my firm faith.

Pan. Nay, I'll give my word for her too: our kindred, though they be long ere they are wooed, they are constant being won: they are burs, I can tell you; they'll stick where they are thrown.

Cres. Boldness comes to me now, and brings me
heart. 120
Prince Troilus, I have loved you night and day
For many weary months.

Tro. Why was my Cressid then so hard to win?

Cres. Hard to seem won: but I was won, my
lord,

With the first glance that ever — pardon me;
If I confess much, you will play the tyrant.
I love you now; but not, till now, so much
But I might master it: in faith, I lie;
My thoughts were like unbridled children, grown
Too headstrong for their mother. See, we fools! 130
Why have I blabb'd? who shall be true to us,
When we are so unsecret to ourselves?
But, though I loved you well, I woo'd you not;
And yet, good faith, I wish'd myself a man,
Or that we women had men's privilege
Of speaking first. Sweet, bid me hold my tongue;
For in this rapture I shall surely speak
The thing I shall repent. See, see, your silence,
Cunning in dumbness, from my weakness draws
My very soul of counsel! Stop my mouth. 140

Tro. And shall, albeit sweet music issues thence.

Pan. Pretty, i' faith.

Cres. My lord, I do beseech you, pardon me;
'Twas not my purpose thus to beg a kiss:
I am ashamed; O heavens! what have I done?
For this time will I take my leave, my lord.

Tro. Your leave, sweet Cressid?

Pan. Leave! an you take leave till to-morrow morning —

Cres. Pray you, content you.

Tro. What offends you, lady? 150

Cres. Sir, mine own company.

Tro. You cannot shun yourself.

Cres. Let me go and try:
I have a kind of self resides with you,
But an unkind self that itself will leave

To be another's fool. I would be gone:
Where is my wit? I know not what I speak.

Tro. Well know they what they speak that speak so wisely.

Cres. Perchance, my lord, I show more craft than love,
And fell so roundly to a large confession 160
To angle for your thoughts: but you are wise;
Or else you love not, for to be wise and love
Exceeds man's might; that dwells with gods above.

Tro. O that I thought it could be in a woman —
As, if it can, I will presume in you —
To feed for aye her lamp and flames of love;
To keep her constancy in plight and youth,
Outliving beauty's outward, with a mind
That doth renew swifter than blood decays!
Or that persuasion could but thus convince me, 170
That my integrity and truth to you
Might be affronted with the match and weight
Of such a winnowed purity in love;
How were I then uplifted! but, alas!
I am as true as truth's simplicity,
And simpler than the infancy of truth.

Cres. In that I'll war with you.

Tro. O virtuous fight,
When right with right wars who shall be most right!
True swains in love shall in the world to come
Approve their truths by Troilus: when their rhymes, 180
Full of protest, of oath and big compare,
Want similes, truth tired with iteration,
'As true as steel, as plantage to the moon,
As sun to day, as turtle to her mate,

As iron to adamant, as earth to the centre,'
Yet, after all comparisons of truth,
As truth's authentic author to be cited,
'As true as Troilus' shall crown up the verse
And sanctify the numbers.

Cres. Prophet may you be!
If I be false, or swerve a hair from truth, 190
When time is old and hath forgot itself,
When waterdrops have worn the stones of Troy,
And blind oblivion swallow'd cities up,
And mighty states characterless are grated
To dusty nothing, yet let memory,
From false to false, among false maids in love,
Upbraid my falsehood! when they've said 'as false
As air, as water, wind, or sandy earth,
As fox to lamb, or wolf to heifer's calf,
Pard to the hind, or stepdame to her son,' 200
'Yea,' let them say, to stick the heart of falsehood,
'As false as Cressid.'

Pan. Go to, a bargain made: seal it, seal it; I'll be the witness. Here I hold your hand; here my cousin's. If ever you prove false one to another, since I have taken such pains to bring you together, let all pitiful goers-between be called to the world's end after my name; call them all Pandars; let all constant men be Troiluses, all false women Cressids, and all brokers-between 210 Panders! Say 'amen.'

Tro. Amen.

Cres. Amen.

Pan. Amen. Whereupon I will show you a chamber with a bed; which bed, because it shall

not speak of your pretty encounters, press it to death: away! [*Exeunt Tro. and Cres.*
And Cupid grant all tongue-tied maidens here
Bed, chamber, Pandar to provide this gear!
[*Exit.*

SCENE III — *The Grecian camp*

Flourish. Enter AGAMEMNON, ULYSSES, DIOMEDES, NESTOR, AJAX, MENELAUS, *and* CALCHAS

Cal. Now, princes, for the service I have done you,
The advantage of the time prompts me aloud
To call for recompense. Appear it to your mind
That, through the sight I bear in things to love,
I have abandon'd Troy, left my possession,
Incurr'd a traitor's name; exposed myself,
From certain and possess'd conveniences,
To doubtful fortunes; sequestering from me all
That time, acquaintance, custom and condition
Made tame and most familiar to my nature, 10
And here, to do you service, am become
As new into the world, strange, unacquainted:
I do beseech you, as in way of taste,
To give me now a little benefit,
Out of those many register'd in promise,
Which, you say, live to come in my behalf.
Agam. What wouldst thou of us, Trojan? make demand.
Cal. You have a Trojan prisoner, call'd Antenor,
Yesterday took: Troy holds him very dear.
Oft have you — often have you thanks therefore — 20
Desired my Cressid in right great exchange,

Whom Troy hath still denied: but this Antenor,
I know, is such a wrest in their affairs,
That their negotiations all must slack,
Wanting his manage; and they will almost
Give us a prince of blood, a son of Priam,
In change of him: let him be sent, great princes,
And he shall buy my daughter; and her presence
Shall quite strike off all service I have done,
In most accepted pain.

Agam. Let Diomedes bear him, 30
And bring us Cressid hither: Calchas shall have
What he requests of us. Good Diomed,
Furnish you fairly for this interchange:
Withal, bring word if Hector will to-morrow
Be answer'd in his challenge: Ajax is ready.

Dio. This shall I undertake; and 'tis a burthen
Which I am proud to bear.

[*Exeunt Diomedes and Calchas.*

Enter ACHILLES *and* PATROCLUS, *before their tent*

Ulyss. Achilles stands i' the entrance of his tent:
Please it our general to pass strangely by him,
As if he were forgot; and, princes all, 40
Lay negligent and loose regard upon him:
I will come last. 'Tis like he'll question me
Why such unplausive eyes are bent on him:
If so, I have derision medicinable,
To use between your strangeness and his pride,
Which his own will shall have desire to drink.
It may do good: pride hath no other glass
To show itself but pride, for supple knees
Feed arrogance and are the proud man's fees.

Agam. We'll execute your purpose and put on 50
A form of strangeness as we pass along;
So do each lord, and either greet him not
Or else disdainfully, which shall shake him more
Than if not look'd on. I will lead the way.

Achil. What, comes the general to speak with me?
You know my mind; I'll fight no more 'gainst Troy.

Agam. What says Achilles? would he aught with us?

Nest. Would you, my lord, aught with the general?

Achil. No.

Nest. Nothing, my lord. 60

Agam. The better.

[*Exeunt Agamemnon and Nestor.*

Achil. Good day, good day.

Men. How do you? how do you? [*Exit.*

Achil. What, does the cuckold scorn me?

Ajax. How now, Patroclus!

Achil. Good morning, Ajax.

Ajax. Ha?

Achil. Good morrow.

Ajax. Ay, and good next day too. [*Exit.*

Achil. What mean these fellows? Know they not Achilles? 70

Patr. They pass by strangely: they were used to bend,
To send their smiles before them to Achilles,
To come as humbly as they used to creep
To holy altars.

Achil. What, am I poor of late?
'Tis certain, greatness, once fall'n out with fortune,

Must fall out with men too: what the declined is,
He shall as soon read in the eyes of others
As feel in his own fall: for men, like butterflies,
Show not their mealy wings but to the summer;
And not a man, for being simply man, 80
Hath any honour, but honour for those honours
That are without him, as place, riches, and favour,
Prizes of accident as oft as merit:
Which when they fall, as being slippery standers,
The love that lean'd on them as slippery too,
Do one pluck down another and together
Die in the fall. But 'tis not so with me:
Fortune and I are friends: I do enjoy
At ample point all that I did possess,
Save these men's looks; who do, methinks, find out 90
Something not worth in me such rich beholding
As they have often given. Here is Ulysses:
I'll interrupt his reading.
How now, Ulysses!

Ulyss. Now, great Thetis' son!

Achil. What are you reading?

Ulyss. A strange fellow here
Writes me: 'That man, how dearly ever parted,
How much in having, or without or in,
Cannot make boast to have that which he hath,
Nor feels not what he owes, but by reflection;
As when his virtues shining upon others 100
Heat them, and they retort that heat again
To the first giver.'

Achil. This is not strange, Ulysses.
The beauty that is borne here in the face
The bearer knows not, but commends itself

To others' eyes: nor doth the eye itself,
That most pure spirit of sense, behold itself,
Not going from itself; but eye to eye opposed
Salutes each other with each other's form:
For speculation turns not to itself,
Till it hath travell'd and is mirror'd there 110
Where it may see itself. This is not strange at all.

Ulyss. I do not strain at the position —
It is familiar — but at the author's drift;
Who in his circumstance expressly proves
That no man is the lord of any thing,
Though in and of him there be much consisting,
Till he communicate his parts to others;
Nor doth he of himself know them for aught,
Till he behold them formed in the applause
Where they're extended; who, like an arch, rever-
berates 120
The voice again; or, like a gate of steel
Fronting the sun, receives and renders back
His figure and his heat. I was much rapt in this;
And apprehended here immediately
The unknown Ajax.
Heavens, what a man is there! a very horse;
That has he knows not what. Nature, what things
there are,
Most abject in regard and dear in use!
What things again most dear in the esteem
And poor in worth! Now shall we see to-morrow — 130
An act that very chance doth throw upon him —
Ajax renown'd. O heavens, what some men do,
While some men leave to do!
How some men creep in skittish fortune's hall,

Whiles others play the idiots in her eyes!
How one man eats into another's pride,
While pride is fasting in his wantonness!
To see these Grecian lords! Why, even already
They clap the lubber Ajax on the shoulder,
As if his foot were on brave Hector's breast 140
And great Troy shrieking.

Achil. I do believe it; for they pass'd by me
As misers do by beggars, neither gave to me
Good word nor look: what, are my deeds forgot?

Ulyss. Time hath, my lord, a wallet at his back
Wherein he puts alms for oblivion,
A great-sized monster of ingratitudes:
Those scraps are good deeds past, which are devour'd
As fast as they are made, forgot as soon
As done: perseverance, dear my lord, 150
Keeps honour bright: to have done, is to hang
Quite out of fashion, like a rusty mail
In monumental mockery. Take the instant way;
For honour travels in a strait so narrow,
Where one but goes abreast: keep then the path;
For emulation hath a thousand sons
That one by one pursue: if you give way,
Or hedge aside from the direct forthright,
Like to an enter'd tide they all rush by
And leave you hindmost: 160
Or, like a gallant horse fall'n in first rank,
Lie there for pavement to the abject rear,
O'er-run and trampled on: then what they do in
present,
Though less than yours in past, must o'ertop yours;
For time is like a fashionable host

That slightly shakes his parting guest by the hand,
And with his arms outstretch'd, as he would fly,
Grasps in the comer: welcome ever smiles,
And farewell goes out sighing. O, let not virtue seek
Remuneration for the thing it was; 170
For beauty, wit,
High birth, vigour of bone, desert in service,
Love, friendship, charity, are subjects all
To envious and calumniating time.
One touch of nature makes the whole world kin;
That all with one consent praise new-born gawds,
Though they are made and moulded of things past,
And give to dust that is a little gilt
More laud than gilt o'er-dusted.
The present eye praises the present object: 180
Then marvel not, thou great and complete man,
That all the Greeks begin to worship Ajax;
Since things in motion sooner catch the eye
Than what not stirs. The cry went once on thee,
And still it might, and yet it may again,
If thou wouldst not entomb thyself alive
And case thy reputation in thy tent,
Whose glorious deeds, but in these fields of late,
Made emulous missions 'mongst the gods themselves,
And drave great Mars to faction.

Achil. Of this my privacy 190
I have strong reasons.

Ulyss. But 'gainst your privacy
The reasons are more potent and heroical:
'Tis known, Achilles, that you are in love
With one of Priam's daughters.

Achil. Ha! known?

Ulyss. Is that a wonder?
The providence that's in a watchful state
Knows almost every grain of Plutus' gold,
Finds bottom in the uncomprehensive deeps,
Keeps place with thought, and almost like the gods
Does thoughts unveil in their dumb cradles. 200
There is a mystery, with whom relation
Durst never meddle, in the soul of state;
Which hath an operation more divine
Than breath or pen can give expressure to:
All the commerce that you have had with Troy
As perfectly is ours as yours, my lord;
And better would it fit Achilles much
To throw down Hector than Polyxena:
But it must grieve young Pyrrhus now at home,
When fame shall in our islands sound her trump; 210
And all the Greekish girls shall tripping sing
'Great Hector's sister did Achilles win,
But our great Ajax bravely beat down him.'
Farewell, my lord: I as your lover speak;
The fool slides o'er the ice that you should break.
[*Exit.*

Patr. To this effect, Achilles, have I moved you:
A woman impudent and mannish grown
Is not more loathed than an effeminate man
In time of action. I stand condemn'd for this;
They think my little stomach to the war 220
And your great love to me restrains you thus:
Sweet, rouse yourself, and the weak wanton Cupid
Shall from your neck unloose his armorous fold,
And, like a dew-drop from the lion's mane,
Be shook to air.

Achil. Shall Ajax fight with Hector?

Patr. Ay, and perhaps receive much honour by him.

Achil. I see my reputation is at stake;
My fame is shrewdly gored.

Patr. O, then, beware;
Those wounds heal ill that men do give themselves:
Omission to do what is necessary 230
Seals a commission to a blank of danger;
And danger, like an ague, subtly taints
Even then when we sit idly in the sun.

Achil. Go call Thersites hither, sweet Patroclus:
I'll send the fool to Ajax, and desire him
To invite the Trojan lords after the combat
To see us here unarm'd: I have a woman's longing,
An appetite that I am sick withal,
To see great Hector in his weeds of peace;
To talk with him, and to behold his visage, 240
Even to my full of view. — A labour saved!

Enter THERSITES

Ther. A wonder!

Achil. What?

Ther. Ajax goes up and down the field, asking for himself.

Achil. How so?

Ther. He must fight singly to-morrow with Hector, and is so prophetically proud of an heroical cudgelling that he raves in saying nothing.

Achil. How can that be? 250

Ther. Why, a' stalks up and down like a peacock, — astride and a stand: ruminates like an hostess that hath no arithmetic but her brain to set down her reckoning: bites his lip with a politic regard, as who should say 'There were wit in this head, an 'twould out:' and so there is; but it lies as coldly in him as fire in a flint, which will not show without knocking. The man's undone for ever; for if Hector break not his neck i' the combat, he'll break 't himself in vain-glory. He knows 260 not me: I said 'Good morrow, Ajax;' and he replies 'Thanks, Agamemnon.' What think you of this man, that takes me for the general? He's grown a very land-fish, languageless, a monster. A plague of opinion! a man may wear it on both sides like a leather jerkin.

Achil. Thou must be my ambassador to him, Thersites.

Ther. Who, I? why, he'll answer nobody; he professes not answering: speaking is for beggars; 270 he wears his tongue in his arms. I will put on his presence: let Patroclus make demands to me, you shall see the pageant of Ajax.

Achil. To him, Patroclus: tell him I humbly desire the valiant Ajax to invite the most valorous Hector to come unarmed to my tent, and to procure safe-conduct for his person of the magnanimous and most illustrious six-or-seven-times-honoured captain-general of the Grecian army, Agamemnon, et cetera. Do this. 280

Patr. Jove bless great Ajax!

Ther. Hum!

Patr. I come from the worthy Achilles, —

Ther. Ha!

Patr. Who most humbly desires you to invite Hector to his tent, —

Ther. Hum!

Patr. And to procure safe-conduct from Agamemnon.

Ther. Agamemnon? 290

Patr. Ay, my lord.

Ther. Ha!

Patr. What say you to 't?

Ther. God be wi' you, with all my heart.

Patr. Your answer, sir.

Ther. If to-morrow be a fair day, by eleven of the clock it will go one way or other: howsoever, he shall pay for me ere he has me.

Patr. Your answer, sir.

Ther. Fare you well, with all my heart. 300

Achil. Why, but he is not in this tune, is he?

Ther. No, but he's out o' tune thus. What music will be in him when Hector has knocked out his brains, I know not; but, I am sure, none, unless the fiddler Apollo get his sinews to make catlings on.

Achil. Come, thou shalt bear a letter to him straight.

Ther. Let me bear another to his horse; for that's the more capable creature.

Achil. My mind is troubled like a fountain stirr'd, 310
And I myself see not the bottom of it.

[*Exeunt Achilles and Patroclus.*

Ther. Would the fountain of your mind were clear again, that I might water an ass at it! I had rather be a tick in a sheep than such a valiant ignorance. [*Exit.*

ACT IV

SCENE I — *Troy. A street*

Enter, at one side, ÆNEAS, *and* Servant *with a torch; at the other,* PARIS, DEIPHOBUS, ANTENOR, DIOMEDES, *and others, with torches*

Par. See, ho! who is that there?
Dei. It is the Lord Æneas.
Æne. Is the prince there in person?
Had I so good occasion to lie long
As you, Prince Paris, nothing but heavenly business
Should rob my bed-mate of my company.
Dio. That's my mind too. Good morrow, Lord Æneas.
Par. A valiant Greek, Æneas, — take his hand, —
Witness the process of your speech, wherein
You told how Diomed a whole week by days 10
Did haunt you in the field.
Æne. Health to you, valiant sir,
During all question of the gentle truce;
But when I meet you arm'd, as black defiance
As heart can think or courage execute.
Dio. The one and other Diomed embraces.
Our bloods are now in calm; and, so long, health;
But when contention and occasion meet,
By Jove, I'll play the hunter for thy life
With all my force, pursuit and policy. 20
Æne. And thou shalt hunt a lion, that will fly
With his face backward. In humane gentleness,
Welcome to Troy! now, by Anchises' life,
Welcome, indeed! By Venus' hand I swear,

No man alive can love in such a sort
The thing he means to kill more excellently.
Dio. We sympathise. Jove, let Æneas live,
If to my sword his fate be not the glory,
A thousand complete courses of the sun!
But, in mine emulous honour, let him die, 30
With every joint a wound, and that to-morrow.
Æne. We know each other well.
Dio. We do; and long to know each other worse.
Par. This is the most despiteful gentle greeting,
The noblest hateful love, that e'er I heard of.
What business, lord, so early?
Æne. I was sent for to the king; but why, I know not.
Par. His purpose meets you: 'twas to bring this Greek
To Calchas' house; and there to render him,
For the enfreed Antenor, the fair Cressid: 40
Let's have your company, or, if you please,
Haste there before us. I constantly do think,
Or rather, call my thought a certain knowledge,
My brother Troilus lodges there to-night:
Rouse him and give him note of our approach,
With the whole quality wherefore: I fear
We shall be much unwelcome.
Æne. That I assure you:
Troilus had rather Troy were borne to Greece
Than Cressid borne from Troy.
Par. There is no help;
The bitter disposition of the time 50
Will have it so. On, lord, we'll follow you.

Æne. Good morrow, all. [*Exit with Servant.*

Par. And tell me, noble Diomed, faith, tell me true,
Even in the soul of sound good-fellowship,
Who, in your thoughts, deserves fair Helen best,
Myself or Menelaus?

Dio. Both alike:
He merits well to have her that doth seek her,
Not making any scruple of her soilure,
With such a hell of pain and world of charge,
And you as well to keep her, that defend her, 60
Not palating the taste of her dishonour,
With such a costly loss of wealth and friends:
He, like a puling cuckold, would drink up
The lees and dregs of a flat tamed piece;
You, like a lecher, out of whorish loins
Are pleased to breed out your inheritors:
Both merits poised, each weighs nor less nor more,
But he as he, the heavier for a whore.

Par. You are too bitter to your countrywoman.

Dio. She's bitter to her country; hear me, Paris: 70
For every false drop in her bawdy veins
A Grecian's life hath sunk; for every scruple
Of her contaminated carrion weight,
A Trojan hath been slain: since she could speak,
She hath not given so many good words breath
As for her Greeks and Trojans suffer'd death.

Par. Fair Diomed, you do as chapmen do,
Dispraise the thing that you desire to buy:
But we in silence hold this virtue well,
We'll not commend what we intend to sell. 80
Here lies our way. [*Exeunt.*

SCENE II — *Court of Pandarus' house*

Enter TROILUS *and* CRESSIDA

Tro. Dear, trouble not yourself: the morn is cold.

Cres. Then, sweet my lord, I'll call mine uncle down;
He shall unbolt the gates.

Tro. Trouble him not;
To bed, to bed: sleep kill those pretty eyes,
And give as soft attachment to thy senses
As infants' empty of all thought!

Cres. Good morrow, then.

Tro. I prithee now, to bed.

Cres. Are you a-weary of me?

Tro. O Cressida! but that the busy day,
Waked by the lark, hath roused the ribald crows,
And dreaming night will hide our joys no longer, 10
I would not from thee.

Cres. Night hath been too brief.

Tro. Beshrew the witch! with venomous wights she stays
As tediously as hell, but flies the grasps of love
With wings more momentary-swift than thought.
You will catch cold, and curse me.

Cres. Prithee, tarry:
You men will never tarry.
O foolish Cressid! I might have still held off,
And then you would have tarried. Hark! there's one up.

Pan. [*Within*] What, 's all the doors open here?

Tro. It is your uncle. 20

Cres. A pestilence on him! now will he be mocking: I shall have such a life!

Enter PANDARUS

Pan. How now, how now! how go maidenheads? Here, you maid! where's my cousin Cressid?

Cres. Go hang yourself, you naughty mocking uncle!
You bring me to do — and then you flout me too.

Pan. To do what? to do what? let her say what: what have I brought you to do?

Cres. Come, come, beshrew your heart! you'll ne'er be good, nor suffer others. 30

Pan. Ha, ha! Alas, poor wretch! ah, poor capocchia! hast not slept to-night? would he not, a naughty man, let it sleep? a bugbear take him!

Cres. Did not I tell you? would he were knock'd i' the head! [*One knocks.*
Who's that at door? good uncle, go and see.
My lord, come you again into my chamber.
You smile and mock me, as if I meant naughtily.

Tro. Ha, ha!

Cres. Come, you are deceived, I think of no such thing. [*Knocking.*
How earnestly they knock! Pray you, come in: 40
I would not for half Troy have you seen here.
[*Exeunt Troilus and Cressida.*

Pan. Who's there? what's the matter? will you beat down the door? How now! what's the matter?

Enter ÆNEAS

Æne. Good morrow, lord, good morrow.

Pan. Who's there? my lord Æneas! By my troth, I knew you not: what news with you so early?

Æne. Is not prince Troilus here?

Pan. Here! what should he do here?

Æne. Come, he is here, my lord; do not deny him: 50

It doth import him much to speak with me.

Pan. Is he here, say you? 'tis more than I know, I'll be sworn: for my own part, I came in late. What should he do here?

Æne. Who! nay, then: come, come, you'll do him wrong ere you are ware: you'll be so true to him, to be false to him: do not you know of him, but yet go fetch him hither; go.

Re-enter TROILUS

Tro. How now! what's the matter?

Æne. My lord, I scarce have leisure to salute you, 60
My matter is so rash: there is at hand
Paris your brother and Deiphobus,
The Grecian Diomed, and our Antenor
Deliver'd to us; and for him forthwith,
Ere the first sacrifice, within this hour,
We must give up to Diomedes' hand
The Lady Cressida.

Tro. Is it so concluded?

Æne. By Priam and the general state of Troy:
They are at hand and ready to effect it.

Tro. How my achievements mock me! 70
I will go meet them: and, my Lord Æneas,
We met by chance: you did not find me here.

Æne. Good, good, my lord; the secrets of nature
Have not more gift in taciturnity.

[*Exeunt Troilus and Æneas.*

Pan. Is 't possible? no sooner got but lost? The devil take Antenor! the young prince will go mad: a plague upon Antenor! I would they had broke 's neck!

Re-enter CRESSIDA

Cres. How now! what's the matter? who was here? 80

Pan. Ah, ah!

Cres. Why sigh you so profoundly? where's my lord? gone! Tell me, sweet uncle, what's the matter?

Pan. Would I were as deep under the earth as I am above!

Cres. O the gods! What's the matter?

Pan. Prithee, get thee in: would thou hadst ne'er been born! I knew thou wouldst be his death: O, poor gentleman! A plague upon Antenor! 90

Cres. Good uncle, I beseech you, on my knees I beseech you, what's the matter?

Pan. Thou must be gone, wench, thou must be gone; thou art changed for Antenor: thou must to thy father, and be gone from Troilus: 'twill be his death; 'twill be his bane; he cannot bear it.

Cres. O you immortal gods! I will not go.

Pan. Thou must.

Cres. I will not, uncle: I have forgot my father;
I know no touch of consanguinity; 100
No kin, no love, no blood, no soul so near me
As the sweet Troilus. O you gods divine!
Make Cressid's name the very crown of falsehood,
If ever she leave Troilus! Time, force, and death,

Do to this body what extremes you can;
But the strong base and building of my love
Is as the very centre of the earth,
Drawing all things to it. I'll go in and weep, —

Pan. Do, do.

Cres. Tear my bright hair and scratch my praised cheeks, 110
Crack my clear voice with sobs, and break my heart
With sounding Troilus. I will not go from Troy.
[*Exeunt.*

SCENE III — *Before Pandarus' house*

Enter PARIS, TROILUS, ÆNEAS, DEIPHOBUS, ANTENOR, *and* DIOMEDES

Par. It is great morning, and the hour prefix'd
For her delivery to this valiant Greek
Comes fast upon: good my brother Troilus,
Tell you the lady what she is to do,
And haste her to the purpose.

Tro. Walk into her house;
I'll bring her to the Grecian presently:
And to his hand when I deliver her,
Think it an altar, and thy brother Troilus
A priest, there offering to it his own heart. [*Exit.*

Par. I know what 'tis to love; 10
And would, as I shall pity, I could help!
Please you walk in, my lords. [*Exeunt.*

SCENE IV — *A room in Pandarus' house*

Enter PANDARUS *and* CRESSIDA

Pan. Be moderate, be moderate.

Cres. Why tell you me of moderation?

The grief is fine, full, perfect, that I taste.
And violenteth in a sense as strong
As that which causeth it: how can I moderate it?
If I could temporise with my affection,
Or brew it to a weak and colder palate,
The like allayment could I give my grief:
My love admits no qualifying dross;
No more my grief, in such a precious loss. 10

Enter TROILUS

Pan. Here, here, here he comes. Ah, sweet ducks!

Cres. O Troilus! Troilus! [*Embracing him.*

Pan. What a pair of spectacles is here! Let me embrace too. 'O heart,' as the goodly saying is,

'O heart, heavy heart,
Why sigh'st thou without breaking?'

where he answers again,

'Because thou canst not ease thy smart
By friendship nor by speaking.' 20

There was never a truer rhyme. Let us cast away nothing, for we may live to have need of such a verse: we see it, we see it. How now, lambs!

Tro. Cressid, I love thee in so strain'd a purity,
That the blest gods, as angry with my fancy,
More bright in zeal than the devotion which
Cold lips blow to their deities, take thee from me.

Cres. Have the gods envy?

Pan. Ay, ay, ay, ay; 'tis too plain a case.

Cres. And is it true that I must go from Troy? 30

Tro. A hateful truth.
Cres. What, and from Troilus too?
Tro. From Troy and Troilus.
Cres. Is it possible?
Tro. And suddenly; where injury of chance
Puts back leave-taking, justles roughly by
All time of pause, rudely beguiles our lips
Of all rejoindure, forcibly prevents
Our lock'd embrasures, strangles our dear vows
Even in the birth of our own labouring breath:
We two, that with so many thousand sighs
Did buy each other, must poorly sell ourselves 40
With the rude brevity and discharge of one.
Injurious time now with a robber's haste
Crams his rich thievery up, he knows not how:
As many farewells as be stars in heaven,
With distinct breath and consign'd kisses to them,
He fumbles up into a loose adieu,
And scants us with a single famish'd kiss,
Distasted with the salt of broken tears.
Æne. [*Within*] My lord, is the lady ready?
Tro. Hark! you are call'd: some say the Genius so 50
Cries 'Come!' to him that instantly must die.
Bid them have patience; she shall come anon.
Pan. Where are my tears? rain, to lay this wind, or my heart will be blown up by the root. [*Exit.*
Cres. I must then to the Grecians?
Tro. No remedy.
Cres. A woeful Cressid 'mongst the merry Greeks!
When shall we see again?
Tro. Hear me, my love: be thou but true of heart,—

Cres. I true! how now! what wicked deem is this?

Tro. Nay, we must use expostulation kindly, 60
For it is parting from us:
I speak not 'be thou true,' as fearing thee;
For I will throw my glove to Death himself,
That there's no maculation in thy heart:
But 'be thou true' say I, to fashion in
My sequent protestation; be thou true,
And I will see thee.

Cres. O, you shall be exposed, my lord, to dangers
As infinite as imminent: but I'll be true.

Tro. And I'll grow friend with danger. Wear this sleeve. 70

Cres. And you this glove. When shall I see you?

Tro. I will corrupt the Grecian sentinels,
To give thee nightly visitation.
But yet, be true.

Cres. O heavens! 'Be true' again!

Tro. Hear why I speak it, love:
The Grecian youths are full of quality;
They're loving, well composed with gifts of nature,
Flowing and swelling o'er with arts and exercise:
How novelty may move, and parts with person,
Alas, a kind of godly jealousy— 80
Which, I beseech you, call a virtuous sin —
Makes me afeard.

Cres. O heavens! you love me not.

Tro. Die I a villain then!
In this I do not call your faith in question,
So mainly as my merit: I cannot sing,
Nor heel the high lavolt, nor sweeten talk,

Nor play at subtle games; fair virtues all,
To which the Grecians are most prompt and preg-
nant:
But I can tell that in each grace of these
There lurks a still and dumb-discoursive devil 90
That tempts most cunningly: but be not tempted.

Cres. Do you think I will?

Tro. No:
But something may be done that we will not:
And sometimes we are devils to ourselves,
When we will tempt the frailty of our powers,
Presuming on their changeful potency.

Æne. [*Within*] Nay, good my lord!

Tro. Come, kiss; and let us part.

Par. [*Within*] Brother Troilus!

Tro. Good brother, come you hither;
And bring Æneas and the Grecian with you. 100

Cres. My lord, will you be true?

Tro. Who, I? alas, it is my vice, my fault:
Whiles others fish with craft for great opinion,
I with great truth catch mere simplicity;
Whilst some with cunning gild their copper crowns,
With truth and plainness I do wear mine bare.
Fear not my truth: the moral of my wit
Is 'plain and true'; there's all the reach of it.

Enter ÆNEAS, PARIS, ANTENOR, DEIPHOBUS, *and* DIOMEDES

Welcome, Sir Diomed! here is the lady
Which for Antenor we deliver you: 110
At the port, lord, I'll give her to thy hand;
And by the way possess thee what she is.
Entreat her fair; and, by my soul, fair Greek,

If e'er thou stand at mercy of my sword,
Name Cressid, and thy life shall be as safe
As Priam is in Ilion.

Dio. Fair Lady Cressid,
So please you, save the thanks this prince expects:
The lustre in your eye, heaven in your cheek,
Pleads your fair usage; and to Diomed
You shall be mistress, and command him wholly. 120

Tro. Grecian, thou dost not use me courteously,
To shame the zeal of my petition to thee
In praising her: I tell thee, lord of Greece,
She is far high-soaring o'er thy praises
As thou unworthy to be call'd her servant.
I charge thee use her well, even for my charge;
For, by the dreadful Pluto, if thou dost not,
Though the great bulk Achilles be thy guard,
I'll cut thy throat.

Dio. O, be not moved, Prince Troilus:
Let me be privileged by my place and message 130
To be a speaker free; when I am hence,
I'll answer to my lust: and know you, lord,
I'll nothing do on charge: to her own worth
She shall be prized; but that you say 'Be 't so,'
I'll speak it in my spirit and honour 'No!'

Tro. Come, to the port. I'll tell thee, Diomed,
This brave shall oft make thee to hide thy head.
Lady, give me your hand; and, as we walk,
To our own selves bend we our needful talk.

[*Exeunt Troilus, Cressida, and Diomedes.*

[*A trumpet sounds.*

Par. Hark! Hector's trumpet.

Æne. How have we spent this morning! 140

The prince must think me tardy and remiss,
That swore to ride before him to the field.

Par. 'Tis Troilus' fault: come, come, to field with him.

Dei. Let us make ready straight.

Æne. Yea, with a bridegroom's fresh alacrity,
Let us address to tend on Hector's heels:
The glory of our Troy doth this day lie
On his fair worth and single chivalry. [*Exeunt.*

SCENE V — *The Grecian camp. Lists set out*

Enter AJAX, *armed;* AGAMEMNON, ACHILLES, PATROCLUS, MENELAUS, ULYSSES, NESTOR, *and others*

Agam. Here art thou in appointment fresh and fair,
Anticipating time with starting courage.
Give with thy trumpet a loud note to Troy,
Thou dreadful Ajax, that the appalled air
May pierce the head of the great combatant
And hale him hither.

Ajax. Thou, trumpet, there's my purse.
Now crack thy lungs, and split thy brazen pipe:
Blow, villain, till thy sphered bias cheek
Outswell the colic of puff'd Aquilon:
Come, stretch thy chest, and let thy eyes spout blood; 10
Thou blow'st for Hector. [*Trumpet sounds.*

Ulyss. No trumpet answers.

Achil. 'Tis but early days.

Agam. Is not yond Diomed, with Calchas' daughter?

Ulyss. 'Tis he, I ken the manner of his gait;

He rises on the toe: that spirit of his
In aspiration lifts him from the earth.

Enter DIOMEDES, *with* CRESSIDA

Agam. Is this the Lady Cressid?
Dio. Even she.
Agam. Most dearly welcome to the Greeks, sweet lady.
Nest. Our general doth salute you with a kiss.
Ulyss. Yet is the kindness but particular; 20
'Twere better she were kiss'd in general.
Nest. And very courtly counsel: I'll begin.
So much for Nestor.
Achil. I'll take that winter from your lips, fair lady:
Achilles bids you welcome.
Men. I had good argument for kissing once.
Patr. But that's no argument for kissing now;
For thus popp'd Paris in his hardiment,
And parted thus you and your argument.
Ulyss. O deadly gall, and theme of all our scorns! 30
For which we lose our heads to gild his horns.
Patr. The first was Menelaus' kiss; this, mine:
Patroclus kisses you.
Men. O, this is trim!
Patr. Paris and I kiss evermore for him.
Men. I'll have my kiss, sir. Lady, by your leave.
Cres. In kissing, do you render or receive?
Patr. Both take and give.
Cres. I'll make my match to live,
The kiss you take is better than you give;
Therefore no kiss.

Men. I'll give you boot, I'll give you three for one. 40

Cres. You're an odd man; give even, or give none.

Men. An odd man, lady! every man is odd.

Cres. No, Paris is not; for, you know, 'tis true,
That you are odd, and he is even with you.

Men. You fillip me o' the head.

Cres. No, I'll be sworn.

Ulyss. It were no match, your nail against his horn.
May I, sweet lady, beg a kiss of you?

Cres. You may.

Ulyss. I do desire it.

Cres. Why, beg then.

Ulyss. Why then, for Venus' sake, give me a kiss,
When Helen is a maid again, and his. 50

Cres. I am your debtor; claim it when 'tis due.

Ulyss. Never's my day, and then a kiss of you.

Dio. Lady, a word: I'll bring you to your father.
[*Exit with Cressida.*

Nest. A woman of quick sense.

Ulyss. Fie, fie upon her!
There's language in her eye, her cheek, her lip,
Nay, her foot speaks; her wanton spirits look out
At every joint and motive of her body.
O, these encounterers, so glib of tongue,
That give accosting welcome ere it comes,
And wide unclasp the tables of their thoughts 60
To every ticklish reader! set them down
For sluttish spoils of opportunity,
And daughters of the game. [*Trumpet within.*

note books

All. The Trojans' trumpet.

Agam. Yonder comes the troop.

Flourish. Enter HECTOR, *armed;* ÆNEAS, TROILUS, *and other* Trojans, *with* Attendants

Æne. Hail, all the state of Greece! what shall be done
To him that victory commands? or do you purpose
A victor shall be known? will you the knights
Shall to the edge of all extremity
Pursue each other, or shall they be divided
By any voice or order of the field? 70
Hector bade ask.

Agam. Which way would Hector have it?

Æne. He cares not; he'll obey conditions.

Achil. 'Tis done like Hector; but securely done,
A little proudly, and great deal misprizing
The knight opposed.

Æne. If not Achilles, sir,
What is your name?

Achil. If not Achilles, nothing.

Æne. Therefore Achilles: but, whate'er, know this:
In the extremity of great and little,
Valour and pride excel themselves in Hector;
The one almost as infinite as all, 80
The other blank as nothing. Weigh him well,
And that which looks like pride is courtesy.
This Ajax is half made of Hector's blood:
In love whereof, half Hector stays at home;
Half heart, half hand, half Hector comes to seek
This blended knight, half Trojan and half Greek.

Achil. A maiden battle then? O, I perceive you.

Re-enter DIOMEDES

Agam. Here is Sir Diomed. Go, gentle knight,
Stand by our Ajax: as you and Lord Æneas
Consent upon the order of their fight, 90
So be it; either to the uttermost,
Or else a breath: the combatants being kin
Half stints their strife before their strokes begin.
[*Ajax and Hector enter the lists.*

Ulyss. They are opposed already.

Agam. What Trojan is that same that looks so heavy?

Ulyss. The youngest son of Priam, a true knight,
Not yet mature, yet matchless, firm of word,
Speaking in deeds and deedless in his tongue,
Not soon provoked nor being provoked soon calm'd;
His heart and hand both open and both free; 100
For what he has he gives, what thinks he shows;
Yet gives he not till judgement guide his bounty,
Nor dignifies an impair thought with breath;
Manly as Hector, but more dangerous;
For Hector in his blaze of wrath subscribes
To tender objects, but he in heat of action
Is more vindicative than jealous love:
They call him Troilus, and on him erect
A second hope, as fairly built as Hector.
Thus says Æneas; one that knows the youth 110
Even to his inches, and with private soul
Did in great Ilion thus translate him to me.
[*Alarum. Hector and Ajax fight.*

Agam. They are in action.
Nest. Now, Ajax, hold thine own!
Tro. Hector, thou sleep'st; Awake thee!
Agam. His blows are well disposed: there, Ajax!
Dio. You must no more. [*Trumpets cease.*
Æne. Princes, enough, so please you.
Ajax. I am not warm yet; let us fight again.
Dio. As Hector pleases.
Hect. Why, then will I no more:
Thou art, great lord, my father's sister's son,
A cousin-german to great Priam's seed; 120
The obligation of our blood forbids
A gory emulation 'twixt us twain:
Were thy commixtion Greek and Trojan so,
That thou couldst say 'This hand is Grecian all,
And this is Trojan; the sinews of this leg
All Greek, and this all Troy; my mother's blood
Runs on the dexter cheek, and this sinister
Bounds in my father's;' by Jove multipotent,
Thou shouldst not bear from me a Greekish member
Wherein my sword had not impressure made 130
Of our rank feud: but the just gods gainsay
That any drop thou borrow'dst from thy mother,
My sacred aunt, should by my mortal sword
Be drained! Let me embrace thee, Ajax:
By him that thunders, thou hast lusty arms;
Hector would have them fall upon him thus:
Cousin, all honour to thee!
Ajax. I thank thee, Hector:
Thou art too gentle and too free a man:
I came to kill thee, cousin, and bear hence
A great addition earned in thy death. 140

Hect. Not Neoptolemus so mirable,
On whose bright crest Fame with her loud'st Oyes
Cries 'This is he,' could promise to himself
A thought of added honour torn from Hector.

Æne. There is expectance here from both the sides,
What further you will do.

Hect. We'll answer it;
The issue is embracement: Ajax, farewell.

Ajax. If I might in entreaties find success, —
As seld I have the chance — I would desire
My famous cousin to our Grecian tents. 150

Dio. 'Tis Agamemnon's wish; and great Achilles
Doth long to see unarm'd the valiant Hector.

Hect. Æneas, call my brother Troilus to me:
And signify this loving interview
To the expecters of our Trojan part;
Desire them home. Give me thy hand, my cousin;
I will go eat with thee, and see your knights.

Ajax. Great Agamemnon comes to meet us here.

Hect. The worthiest of them tell me name by name;
But for Achilles, my own searching eyes 160
Shall find him by his large and portly size.

Agam. Worthy of arms! as welcome as to one
That would be rid of such an enemy;
But that's no welcome: understand more clear,
What's past and what's to come is strew'd with husks
And formless ruin of oblivion;
But in this extant moment, faith and troth,
Strain'd purely from all hollow bias-drawing,

Bids thee, with most divine integrity,
From heart of very heart, great Hector, welcome. 170

Hect. I thank thee, most imperious Agamemnon.

Agam. [*To Troilus*] My well-famed lord of Troy, no less to you.

Men. Let me confirm my princely brother's greeting;
You brace of warlike brothers, welcome hither.

Hect. Who must we answer?

Æne. The noble Menelaus.

Hect. O, you, my lord! by Mars his gauntlet, thanks!
Mock not, that I affect the untraded oath;
Your quondam wife swears still by Venus' glove:
She's well, but bade me not commend her to you.

Men. Name her not now, sir; she's a deadly theme. 180

Hect. O, pardon; I offend.

Nest. I have, thou gallant Trojan, seen thee oft,
Labouring for destiny, make cruel way
Through ranks of Greekish youth; and I have seen thee,
As hot as Perseus, spur thy Phrygian steed,
Despising many forfeits and subduements,
When thou hast hung thy advanced sword i' the air,
Not letting it decline on the declined,
That I have said to some my standers by
'Lo, Jupiter is yonder, dealing life!' 190
And I have seen thee pause and take thy breath,
When that a ring of Greeks have hemm'd thee in,
Like an Olympian wrestling: this have I seen;
But this thy countenance, still lock'd in steel,
I never saw till now. I knew thy grandsire,

And once fought with him: he was a soldier good;
But, by great Mars the captain of us all,
Never like thee. Let an old man embrace thee;
And, worthy warrior, welcome to our tents.

Æne. 'Tis the old Nestor. 200

Hect. Let me embrace thee, good old chronicle,
That hast so long walk'd hand in hand with time:
Most reverend Nestor, I am glad to clasp thee.

Nest. I would my arms could match thee in contention,
As they contend with thee in courtesy.

Hect. I would they could.

Nest. Ha!
By this white beard, I'd fight with thee to-morrow:
Well, welcome, welcome! — I have seen the time.

Ulyss. I wonder now how yonder city stands, 210
When we have here her base and pillar by us.

Hect. I know your favour, Lord Ulysses, well.
Ah, sir, there's many a Greek and Trojan dead,
Since first I saw yourself and Diomed
In Ilion, on your Greekish embassy.

Ulyss. Sir, I foretold you then what would ensue:
My prophecy is but half his journey yet;
For yonder walls, that pertly front your town,
Yond towers, whose wanton tops do buss the clouds,
Must kiss their own feet.

Hect. I must not believe you: 220
There they stand yet; and modestly I think,
The fall of every Phrygian stone will cost
A drop of Grecian blood: the end crowns all,
And that old common arbitrator, Time,
Will one day end it.

Ulyss. So to him we leave it.
Most gentle and most valiant Hector, welcome:
After the general, I beseech you next
To feast with me and see me at my tent.
Achil. I shall forestall thee, Lord Ulysses, thou!
Now, Hector, I have fed mine eyes on thee; 230
I have with exact view perused thee, Hector,
And quoted joint by joint.
Hect. Is this Achilles?
Achil. I am Achilles.
Hect. Stand fair, I pray thee: let me look on thee.
Achil. Behold thy fill.
Hect. Nay, I have done already.
Achil. Thou art too brief: I will the second time,
As I would buy thee, view thee limb by limb.
Hect. O, like a book of sport thou'lt read me o'er;
But there's more in me than thou understand'st.
Why dost thou so oppress me with thine eye? 240
Achil. Tell me, you heavens, in which part of his body
Shall I destroy him? whether there, or there, or there?
That I may give the local wound a name,
And make distinct the very breach whereout
Hector's great spirit flew: answer me, heavens!
Hect. It would discredit the blest gods, proud man,
To answer such a question: stand again:
Think'st thou to catch my life so pleasantly,
As to prenominate in nice conjecture
Where thou wilt hit me dead?
Achil. I tell thee, yea. 250

Hect. Wert thou an oracle to tell me so,
I'd not believe thee. Henceforth guard thee well;
For I'll not kill thee there, nor there, nor there;
But, by the forge that stithied Mars his helm,
I'll kill thee every where, yea, o'er and o'er.
You wisest Grecians, pardon me this brag;
His insolence draws folly from my lips;
But I'll endeavour deeds to match these words,
Or may I never —

Ajax. Do not chafe thee, cousin:
And you, Achilles, let these threats alone 260
Till accident or purpose bring you to 't:
You may have every day enough of Hector,
If you have stomach: the general state, I fear,
Can scarce entreat you to be odd with him.

Hect. I pray you, let us see you in the field:
We have had pelting wars since you refused
The Grecians' cause.

Achil. Dost thou entreat me, Hector?
To-morrow do I meet thee, fell as death;
To-night all friends.

Hect. Thy hand upon that match.

Agam. First, all you peers of Greece, go to my tent; 270
There in the full convive we: afterwards,
As Hector's leisure and your bounties shall
Concur together, severally entreat him.
Beat loud the tabourines, let the trumpets blow,
That this great soldier may his welcome know.

[*Exeunt all but Troilus and Ulysses.*

Tro. My Lord Ulysses, tell me, I beseech you,
In what place of the field doth Calchas keep?

Ulyss. At Menelaus' tent, most princely Troilus:
There Diomed doth feast with him to-night;
Who neither looks upon the heaven nor earth, 280
But gives all gaze and bent of amorous view
On the fair Cressid.

Tro. Shall I, sweet lord, be bound to you so much,
After we part from Agamemnon's tent,
To bring me thither?

Ulyss. You shall command me, sir.
As gentle tell me, of what honour was
This Cressida in Troy? Had she no lover there
That wails her absence?

Tro. O, sir, to such as boasting show their scars,
A mock is due. Will you walk on, my lord? 290
She was beloved, she loved; she is, and doth:
But still sweet love is food for fortune's tooth.

[*Exeunt.*

ACT V

Scene I — *The Grecian camp. Before Achilles' tent*

Enter Achilles *and* Patroclus

Achil. I'll heat his blood with Greekish wine to-night,
Which with my scimitar I'll cool to-morrow.
Patroclus, let us feast him to the height.

Patr. Here comes Thersites.

Enter Thersites

Achil. How now, thou core of envy!
Thou crusty batch of nature, what's the news?

Ther. Why, thou picture of what thou seemest,

and idol of idiot-worshippers, here's a letter for thee.

Achil. From whence, fragment?

Ther. Why, thou full dish of fool, from Troy. 10

Patr. Who keeps the tent now?

Ther. The surgeon's box, or the patient's wound.

Patr. Well said, adversity! and what need these tricks?

Ther. Prithee, be silent, boy; I profit not by thy talk: thou art thought to be Achilles' male varlet.

Patr. Male varlet, you rogue! what's that?

Ther. Why, his masculine whore. Now, the rotten diseases of the south, the guts-griping, rup- 20 tures, catarrhs, loads o' gravel i' the back, lethargies, cold palsies, raw eyes, dirt-rotten livers, wheezing lungs, bladders full of imposthume, sciaticas, lime-kilns i' the palm, incurable bone-ache, and the rivelled fee-simple of the tetter, take and take again such preposterous discoveries!

Patr. Why, thou damnable box of envy, thou, what mean'st thou to curse thus?

Ther. Do I curse thee?

Patr. Why, no, you ruinous butt; you whoreson 30 indistinguishable cur, no.

Ther. No! why art thou then exasperate, thou idle immaterial skein of sleave silk, thou green sarcenet flap for a sore eye, thou tassel of a prodigal's purse, thou? Ah, how the poor world is pestered with such waterflies, diminutives of nature!

Patr. Out, gall!

Ther. Finch-egg!

Achil. My sweet Patroclus, I am thwarted quite
From my great purpose in to-morrow's battle. 40
Here is a letter from Queen Hecuba,
A token from her daughter, my fair love,
Both taxing me and gaging me to keep
An oath that I have sworn. I will not break it:
Fall Greeks; fail fame; honour or go or stay;
My major vow lies here, this I'll obey.
Come, come, Thersites, help to trim my tent:
This night in banqueting must all be spent.
Away, Patroclus! [*Exeunt Achilles and Patroclus.*

Ther. With too much blood and too little brain, 50
these two may run mad; but, if with too much
brain and too little blood they do, I'll be a curer
of madmen. Here's Agamemnon, an honest fellow enough and one that loves quails; but he has
not so much brain as ear-wax: and the goodly
transformation of Jupiter there, his brother, the
bull, the primitive statue and oblique memorial
of cuckolds; a thrifty shoeing-horn in a chain,
hanging at his brother's leg, — to what form
but that he is, should wit larded with malice and 60
malice forced with wit turn him to? To an ass,
were nothing; he is both ass and ox: to an ox,
were nothing; he is both ox and ass. To be a dog,
a mule, a cat, a fitchew, a toad, a lizard, an owl,
a puttock, or a herring without a roe, I would
not care; but to be Menelaus! I would conspire
against destiny. Ask me not what I would be,
if I were not Thersites; for I care not to be the
louse of a lazar, so I were not Menelaus. Hoy-day!
spirits and fires! 70

Enter HECTOR, TROILUS, AJAX, AGAMEMNON, ULYSSES, NESTOR, MENELAUS, *and* DIOMEDES, *with lights*

Agam. We go wrong, we go wrong.

Ajax. No, yonder 'tis;
There, where we see the lights.

Hect. I trouble you.

Ajax. No, not a whit.

Re-enter ACHILLES

Ulyss. Here comes himself to guide you.

Achil. Welcome, brave Hector; welcome, princes all.

Agam. So now, fair Prince of Troy, I bid good night.
Ajax commands the guard to tend on you.

Hect. Thanks and good night to the Greeks' general.

Men. Good night, my lord.

Hect. Good night, sweet Lord Menelaus.

Ther. Sweet draught: sweet, quoth a'! sweet sink, sweet sewer. 80

Achil. Good night and welcome, both at once, to those
That go or tarry.

Agam. Good night.

[*Exeunt Agamemnon and Menelaus.*

Achil. Old Nestor tarries; and you too, Diomed,
Keep Hector company an hour or two.

Dio. I cannot, lord; I have important business,
The tide whereof is now. Good night, great Hector.

Hect. Give me your hand.

Ulyss. [*Aside to Troilus*] Follow his torch; he goes to Calchas' tent: 90
I'll keep you company.

Tro. Sweet sir, you honour me.

Hect. And so, good night.

[*Exit Diomedes; Ulysses and Troilus following.*

Achil. Come, come, enter my tent.

[*Exeunt Achilles, Hector, Ajax, and Nestor.*

Ther. That same Diomed's a false-hearted rogue, a most unjust knave; I will no more trust him when he leers than I will a serpent when he hisses: he will spend his mouth and promise, like Brabbler the hound; but when he performs, astronomers foretell it; it is prodigious, there will come some change; the sun borrows of the moon 100 when Diomed keeps his word. I will rather leave to see Hector than not to dog him: they say he keeps a Trojan drab and uses the traitor Calchas' tent: I'll after. Nothing but lechery! all incontinent varlets! [*Exit.*

SCENE II — *The same. Before Calchas' tent*

Enter DIOMEDES

Dio. What, are you up here, ho? speak.

Cal. [*Within*] Who calls?

Dio. Diomed. Calchas, I think. Where's your daughter?

Cal. [*Within*] She comes to you.

Enter TROILUS *and* ULYSSES, *at a distance; after them,* THERSITES

Ulyss. Stand where the torch may not discover us.

Enter CRESSIDA

Tro. Cressid comes forth to him.

Dio. How now, my charge!

Cres. Now, my sweet guardian! Hark, a word with you. [*Whispers.*

Tro. Yea, so familiar!

Ulyss. She will sing any man at first sight.

Ther. And any man may sing her, if he can take her cliff; she's noted. 10

Dio. Will you remember?

Cres. Remember! yes.

Dio. Nay, but do, then;
And let your mind be coupled with your words.

Tro. What should she remember?

Ulyss. List.

Cres. Sweet honey Greek, tempt me no more to folly.

Ther. Roguery!

Dio. Nay, then, — 20

Cres. I'll tell you what, —

Dio. Foh, foh! come, tell a pin: you are forsworn.

Cres. In faith, I cannot: what would you have me do?

Ther. A juggling trick, — to be secretly open.

Dio. What did you swear you would bestow on me?

Cres. I prithee, do not hold me to mine oath;
Bid me do any thing but that, sweet Greek.

Dio. Good night.

Tro. Hold, patience!

Ulyss. How now, Trojan! 30

Cres. Diomed, —

Dio. No, no, good night: I'll be your fool no more.

Tro. Thy better must.

Cres. Hark, one word in your ear.

Tro. O plague and madness!

Ulyss. You are moved, prince; let us depart, I pray you,
Lest your displeasure should enlarge itself
To wrathful terms: this place is dangerous;
The time right deadly; I beseech you, go.

Tro. Behold, I pray you!

Ulyss. Nay, good my lord, go off: 40
You flow to great distraction; come, my lord.

Tro. I pray thee, stay.

Ulyss. You have not patience; come.

Tro. I pray you, stay; by hell and all hell's torments,
I will not speak a word.

Dio. And so, good night.

Cres. Nay, but you part in anger.

Tro. Doth that grieve thee?
O wither'd truth!

Ulyss. Why, how now, lord!

Tro. By Jove,
I will be patient.

Cres. Guardian! — why, Greek!

Dio. Foh, foh! adieu; you palter.

Cres. In faith, I do not: come hither once again.

Ulyss. You shake, my lord, at something: will you go? 50
You will break out.

Tro. She strokes his cheek!

Ulyss. Come, come.

Tro. Nay, stay; by Jove, I will not speak a word:
There is between my will and all offences
A guard of patience: stay a little while.

Ther. How the devil luxury, with his fat rump and potato-finger, tickles these together! Fry, lechery, fry!

Dio. But will you, then?

Cres. In faith, I will, la; never trust me else.

Dio. Give me some token for the surety of it. 60

Cres. I'll fetch you one. [*Exit.*

Ulyss. You have sworn patience.

Tro. Fear me not, sweet lord;
I will not be myself, nor have cognition
Of what I feel: I am all patience.

Re-enter CRESSIDA

Tro. Now the pledge; now, now, now!

Cres. Here, Diomed, keep this sleeve.

Tro. O beauty! where is thy faith?

Ulyss. My lord, —

Tro. I will be patient; outwardly I will.

Cres. You look upon that sleeve; behold it well.
He loved me — O false wench! — Give 't me again. 70

Dio. Whose was 't?

Cres. It is no matter, now I have 't again.
I will not meet with you to-morrow night:
I prithee, Diomed, visit me no more.

Ther. Now she sharpens: well said, whetstone!

Dio. I shall have it.

Cres. What, this?

Dio. Ay, that.

Cres. O, all you gods! O pretty, pretty pledge!
Thy master now lies thinking in his bed
Of thee and me, and sighs, and takes my glove,
And gives memorial dainty kisses to it, 80
As I kiss thee. Nay, do not snatch it from me;
He that takes that doth take my heart withal.

Dio. I had your heart before; this follows it.

Tro. I did swear patience.

Cres. You shall not have it, Diomed; faith, you shall not;
I'll give you something else.

Dio. I will have this: whose was it?

Cres. It is no matter.

Dio. Come, tell me whose it was.

Cres. 'Twas one's that loved me better than you will.
But, now you have it, take it.

Dio. Whose was it? 90

Cres. By all Diana's waiting-women yond,
And by herself, I will not tell you whose.

Dio. To-morrow will I wear it on my helm,
And grieve his spirit that dares not challenge it.

Tro. Wert thou the devil, and worest it on thy horn,
It should be challenged.

Cres. Well, well, 'tis done, 'tis past; and yet it is not;
I will not keep my word.

Dio. Why then, farewell;
Thou never shalt mock Diomed again.

Cres. You shall not go: one cannot speak a word, 100
But it straight starts you.
Dio. I do not like this fooling.
Ther. Nor I, by Pluto: but that that likes not
you
Pleases me best.
Dio. What, shall I come? the hour?
Cres. Ay, come: O Jove! do come: I shall be
plagued.
Dio. Farewell till then.
Cres. Good night: I prithee, come.
[*Exit Diomedes.*
Troilus, farewell! one eye yet looks on thee,
But with my heart the other eye doth see.
Ah, poor our sex! this fault in us I find,
The error of our eye directs our mind:
What error leads must err; O, then conclude 110
Minds sway'd by eyes are full of turpitude. [*Exit.*
Ther. A proof of strength she could not publish
more,
Unless she said 'My mind is now turn'd whore.'
Ulyss. All's done, my lord.
Tro. It is.
Ulyss. Why stay we then?
Tro. To make a recordation to my soul
Of every syllable that here was spoke.
But if I tell how these two did co-act,
Shall I not lie in publishing a truth?
Sith yet there is a credence in my heart,
An esperance so obstinately strong, 120
That doth invert the attest of eyes and ears;
As if those organs had deceptious functions,

Created only to calumniate.
Was Cressid here?
Ulyss. I cannot conjure, Trojan.
Tro. She was not, sure.
Ulyss. Most sure she was.
Tro. Why, my negation hath no taste of madness.
Ulyss. Nor mine, my lord: Cressid was here but now.
Tro. Let it not be believed for womanhood!
Think, we had mothers; do not give advantage
To stubborn critics, apt without a theme 130
For depravation, to square the general sex
By Cressid's rule: rather think this not Cressid.
Ulyss. What hath she done, prince, that can soil our mothers?
Tro. Nothing at all, unless that this were she.
Ther. Will a' swagger himself out on 's own eyes?
Tro. This she? no, this is Diomed's Cressida:
If beauty have a soul, this is not she;
If souls guide vows, if vows be sanctimonies,
If sanctimony be the gods' delight,
If there be rule in unity itself, 140
This is not she. O madness of discourse,
That cause sets up with and against itself!
Bi-fold authority! where reason can revolt
Without perdition, and loss assume all reason
Without revolt: this is, and is not, Cressid!
Within my soul there doth conduce a fight
Of this strange nature, that a thing inseparate
Divides more wider than the sky and earth;
And yet the spacious breadth of this division
Admits no orifex for a point as subtle 150

As Ariachne's broken woof to enter.
Instance, O instance! strong as Pluto's gates;
Cressid is mine, tied with the bonds of heaven:
Instance, O instance! strong as heaven itself;
The bonds of heaven are slipp'd, dissolved and
 loosed;
And with another knot, five-finger-tied,
The fractions of her faith, orts of her love,
The fragments, scraps, the bits and greasy relics
Of her o'er-eaten faith, are bound to Diomed.
 Ulyss. May worthy Troilus be half attach'd 160
With that which here his passion doth express?
 Tro. Ay, Greek; and that shall be divulged well
In characters as red as Mars his heart
Inflamed with Venus: never did young man fancy
With so eternal and so fix'd a soul.
Hark, Greek: as much as I do Cressid love,
So much by weight hate I her Diomed:
That sleeve is mine that he'll bear on his helm:
Were it a casque composed by Vulcan's skill,
My sword should bite it: not the dreadful spout 170
Which shipmen do the hurricano call,
Constringed in mass by the almighty sun,
Shall dizzy with more clamour Neptune's ear
In his descent, than shall my prompted sword
Falling on Diomed.
 Ther. He'll tickle it for his concupy.
 Tro. O Cressid! O false Cressid! false, false, false!
Let all untruths stand by thy stained name,
And they'll seem glorious.
 Ulyss. O, contain yourself;
Your passion draws ears hither. 180

Enter Æneas

Æne. I have been seeking you this hour, my lord:
Hector by this is arming him in Troy;
Ajax your guard stays to conduct you home.

Tro. Have with you, prince. My courteous lord, adieu.
Farewell, revolted fair! and, Diomed,
Stand fast, and wear a castle on thy head!

Ulyss. I'll bring you to the gates.

Tro. Accept distracted thanks.

[*Exeunt Troilus, Æneas, and Ulysses.*

Ther. Would I could meet that rogue Diomed! I would croak like a raven; I would bode, I would 190 bode. Patroclus will give me any thing for the intelligence of this whore: the parrot will not do more for an almond than he for a commodious drab. Lechery, lechery! still wars and lechery! nothing else holds fashion. A burning devil take them! [*Exit.*

Scene III — *Troy. Before Priam's palace*

Enter Hector *and* Andromache

And. When was my lord so much ungently temper'd,
To stop his ears against admonishment?
Unarm, unarm, and do not fight to-day.

Hect. You train me to offend you; get you in:
By all the everlasting gods, I'll go!

And. My dreams will, sure, prove ominous to the day.

Hect. No more, I say.

Enter CASSANDRA

Cas. Where is my brother Hector?

And. Here, sister; arm'd, and bloody in intent.
Consort with me in loud and dear petition;
Pursue we him on knees; for I have dream'd 10
Of bloody turbulence, and this whole night
Hath nothing been but shapes and forms of slaughter.

Cas. O, 'tis true.

Hect. Ho! bid my trumpet sound!

Cas. No notes of sally, for the heavens, sweet brother.

Hect. Be gone, I say: the gods have heard me swear.

Cas. The gods are deaf to hot and peevish vows:
They are polluted offerings, more abhorr'd
Than spotted livers in the sacrifice.

And. O, be persuaded! do not count it holy
To hurt by being just: it is as lawful, 20
For we would give much, to use violent thefts
And rob in the behalf of charity.

Cas. It is the purpose that makes strong the vow;
But vows to every purpose must not hold;
Unarm, sweet Hector.

Hect. Hold you still, I say;
Mine honour keeps the weather of my fate:
Like every man holds dear; but the dear man
Holds honour far more precious-dear than life.

Enter TROILUS

How now, young man! mean'st thou to fight to-day?

And. Cassandra, call my father to persuade. 30
[*Exit Cassandra.*

Hect. No, faith, young Troilus; doff thy harness, youth:
I am to-day i' the vein of chivalry:
Let grow thy sinews till their knots be strong,
And tempt not yet the brushes of the war.
Unarm thee, go; and doubt thou not, brave boy,
I'll stand to-day for thee and me and Troy.

Tro. Brother, you have a vice of mercy in you,
Which better fits a lion than a man.

Hect. What vice is that, good Troilus? chide me for it.

Tro. When many times the captive Grecian falls, 40
Even in the fan and wind of your fair sword,
You bid them rise and live.

Hect. O, 'tis fair play.

Tro. Fool's play, by heaven, Hector.

Hect. How now! how now!

Tro. For the love of all the gods,
Let's leave the hermit pity with our mother;
And when we have our armours buckled on,
The venom'd vengeance ride upon our swords,
Spur them to ruthful work, rein them from ruth!

Hect. Fie, savage, fie!

Tro. Hector, then 'tis wars.

Hect. Troilus, I would not have you fight to-day. 50

Tro. Who should withhold me?
Not fate, obedience, nor the hand of Mars
Beckoning with fiery truncheon my retire;
Not Priamus and Hecuba on knees,
Their eyes o'ergalled with recourse of tears;
Nor you, my brother, with your true sword drawn,

Opposed to hinder me, should stop my way,
But by my ruin.

Re-enter CASSANDRA, *with* PRIAM

Cas. Lay hold upon him, Priam, hold him fast:
He is thy crutch; now if thou lose thy stay, 60
Thou on him leaning, and all Troy on thee,
Fall all together.

Pri. Come, Hector, come, go back:
Thy wife hath dream'd; thy mother hath had visions;
Cassandra doth foresee: and I myself
Am like a prophet suddenly enrapt,
To tell thee that this day is ominous:
Therefore, come back.

Hect. Æneas is afield;
And I do stand engaged to many Greeks,
Even in the faith of valour, to appear
This morning to them.

Pri. Ay, but thou shalt not go. 70

Hect. I must not break my faith.
You know me dutiful; therefore, dear sir,
Let me not shame respect; but give me leave
To take that course by your consent and voice,
Which you do here forbid me, royal Priam.

Cas. O Priam, yield not to him!

And. Do not, dear father.

Hect. Andromache, I am offended with you:
Upon the love you bear me, get you in.
[*Exit Andromache.*

Tro. This foolish, dreaming, superstitious girl
Makes all these bodements.

Cas. O, farewell, dear Hector! 80
Look, how thou diest! look, how thy eye turns pale!
Look, how thy wounds do bleed at many vents!
Hark, how Troy roars! how Hecuba cries out!
How poor Andromache shrills her dolours forth!
Behold, distraction, frenzy and amazement,
Like witless antics, one another meet,
And all cry 'Hector! Hector's dead! O Hector!'

Tro. Away! away!

Cas. Farewell: yet, soft! Hector, I take my leave:
Thou dost thyself and all our Troy deceive. [*Exit.* 90

Hect. You are amazed, my liege, at her exclaim:
Go in and cheer the town: we'll forth and fight,
Do deeds worth praise and tell you them at night.

Pri. Farewell: the gods with safety stand about thee!

[*Exeunt severally Priam and Hector. Alarum.*

Tro. They are at it, hark! Proud Diomed, believe,
I come to lose my arm, or win my sleeve.

Enter PANDARUS

Pan. Do you hear, my lord? do you hear?

Tro. What now?

Pan. Here's a letter come from yon poor girl.

Tro. Let me read. 100

Pan. A whoreson tisick, a whoreson rascally tisick so troubles me, and the foolish fortune of this girl; and what one thing, what another, that I shall leave you one o' these days: and I have a rheum in mine eyes too, and such an ache in my bones that, unless a man were cursed, I cannot tell what to think on 't. What says she there?

Tro. Words, words, mere words, no matter from the heart;
The effect doth operate another way.
[*Tearing the letter.*
Go, wind, to wind, there turn and change together. 110
My love with words and errors still she feeds,
But edifies another with her deeds. [*Exeunt severally.*

SCENE IV — *The field between Troy and the Grecian camp.*
Alarums. Excursions. Enter THERSITES

Ther. Now they are clapper-clawing one another; I'll go look on. That dissembling abominable varlet, Diomed, has got that same scurvy doting foolish young knave's sleeve of Troy there in his helm: I would fain see them meet; that that same young Trojan ass, that loves the whore there, might send that Greekish whoremasterly villain, with the sleeve, back to the dissembling luxurious drab, of a sleeveless errand. O' the other side, the policy of those crafty swearing 10 rascals, that stale old mouse-eaten dry cheese, Nestor, and that same dog-fox, Ulysses, is not proved worth a blackberry. They set me up in policy that mongrel cur, Ajax, against that dog of as bad a kind, Achilles: and now is the cur Ajax prouder than the cur Achilles, and will not arm to-day; whereupon the Grecians begin to proclaim barbarism, and policy grows into an ill opinion.

Enter Diomedes *and* Troilus

Soft! here comes sleeve, and t'other. 20

Tro. Fly not, for shouldst thou take the river Styx,
I would swim after.

Dio. Thou dost miscall retire:
I do not fly; but advantageous care
Withdrew me from the odds of multitude:
Have at thee!

Ther. Hold thy whore, Grecian! Now for thy whore, Trojan! Now the sleeve, now the sleeve!

[*Exeunt Troilus and Diomedes, fighting.*

Enter Hector

Hect. What art thou, Greek? art thou for Hector's match?
Art thou of blood and honour?

Ther. No, no; I am a rascal; a scurvy railing 30
knave; a very filthy rogue.

Hect. I do believe thee. Live. [*Exit.*

Ther. God-a-mercy, that thou wilt believe me; but a plague break thy neck for frighting me! What's become of the wenching rogues? I think they have swallowed one another: I would laugh at that miracle: yet in a sort lechery eats itself. I'll teach them. [*Exit.*

Scene V — *Another part of the field*

Enter Diomedes *and* Servant

Dio. Go, go, my servant, take thou Troilus' horse;
Present the fair steed to my lady Cressid:

Fellow, commend my service to her beauty;
Tell her I have chastised the amorous Trojan,
And am her knight by proof.

Ser. I go, my lord. [*Exit.*

Enter AGAMEMNON

Agam. Renew, renew! The fierce Polydamas
Hath beat down Menon: bastard Margarelon
Hath Doreus prisoner,
And stands colossus-wise, waving his beam,
Upon the pashed corses of the kings 10
Epistrophus and Cedius: Polyxenes is slain;
Amphimachus and Thoas deadly hurt;
Patroclus ta'en or slain; and Palamedes
Sore hurt and bruised: the dreadful Sagittary
Appals our numbers: haste we, Diomed,
To reinforcement, or we perish all.

Enter NESTOR

Nest. Go, bear Patroclus' body to Achilles,
And bid the snail-paced Ajax arm for shame.
There is a thousand Hectors in the field:
Now here he fights on Galathe his horse, 20
And there lacks work; anon he's there afoot,
And there they fly or die, like scaled sculls
Before the belching whale; then is he yonder,
And there the strawy Greeks, ripe for his edge,
Fall down before him, like the mower's swath:
Here, there and every where he leaves and takes,
Dexterity so obeying appetite
That what he will he does, and does so much
That proof is call'd impossibility.

Enter ULYSSES

Ulyss. O, courage, courage, princes! great Achilles 30
Is arming, weeping, cursing, vowing vengeance:
Patroclus' wounds have roused his drowsy blood,
Together with his mangled Myrmidons,
That noseless, handless, hack'd and chipp'd, come to him,
Crying on Hector. Ajax hath lost a friend,
And foams at mouth, and he is arm'd, and at it,
Roaring for Troilus; who hath done to-day
Mad and fantastic execution,
Engaging and redeeming of himself,
With such a careless force and forceless care, 40
As if that luck, in very spite of cunning,
Bade him win all.

Enter AJAX

Ajax. Troilus! thou coward Troilus! [*Exit.*
Dio. Ay, there, there.
Nest. So, so, we draw together.

Enter ACHILLES

Achil. Where is this Hector?
Come, come, thou boy-queller, show thy face;
Know what it is to meet Achilles angry:
Hector! where's Hector? I will none but Hector.
[*Exeunt.*

SCENE VI — *Another part of the field*

Enter AJAX

Ajax. Troilus, thou coward Troilus, show thy head!

Enter DIOMEDES

Dio. Troilus, I say! where's Troilus?
Ajax. What wouldst thou?
Dio. I would correct him.
Ajax. Were I the general, thou shouldst have my office
Ere that correction. Troilus, I say! what, Troilus!

Enter TROILUS

Tro. O traitor Diomed! Turn thy false face, thou traitor,
And pay thy life thou owest me for my horse.
Dio. Ha, art thou there?
Ajax. I'll fight with him alone: stand, Diomed.
Dio. He is my prize; I will not look upon. 10
Tro. Come both, you cogging Greeks; have at you both! [*Exeunt fighting.*

Enter HECTOR

Hect. Yea, Troilus? O, well fought, my youngest brother!

Enter ACHILLES

Achil. Now do I see thee; ha! have at thee, Hector!
Hect. Pause, if thou wilt.
Achil. I do disdain thy courtesy, proud Trojan:
Be happy that my arms are out of use:
My rest and negligence befriends thee now,
But thou anon shalt hear of me again;
Till when, go seek thy fortune. [*Exit.*
Hect. Fare thee well:

I would have been much more a fresher man, 20
Had I expected thee.

Re-enter TROILUS

How now, my brother!

Tro. Ajax hath ta'en Æneas: shall it be?
No, by the flame of yonder glorious heaven,
He shall not carry him; I'll be ta'en too,
Or bring him off. Fate, hear me what I say!
I reck not though I end my life to-day. [*Exit.*

Enter one in sumptuous armour

Hect. Stand, stand, thou Greek; thou art a goodly mark.
No? wilt thou not? I like thy armour well:
I'll frush it, and unlock the rivets all,
But I'll be master of it. Wilt thou not, beast, abide? 30
Why then, fly on, I'll hunt thee for thy hide.
[*Exeunt.*

SCENE VII — *Another part of the field*

Enter ACHILLES, *with* MYRMIDONS

Achil. Come here about me, you my Myrmidons;
Mark what I say. Attend me where I wheel:
Strike not a stroke, but keep yourselves in breath:
And when I have the bloody Hector found,
Empale him with your weapons round about;
In fellest manner execute your aims.
Follow me, sirs, and my proceedings eye:
It is decreed Hector the great must die. [*Exeunt.*

Enter MENELAUS *and* PARIS, *fighting: then* THERSITES

Ther. The cuckold and the cuckold-maker are at it. Now, bull! now, dog! 'loo, Paris, 'loo! now 10 my double-henned sparrow! 'loo, Paris, 'loo! The bull has the game: ware horns, ho!

[*Exeunt Paris and Menelaus.*

Enter MARGARELON

Mar. Turn, slave, and fight.

Ther. What art thou?

Mar. A bastard son of Priam's.

Ther. I am a bastard too; I love bastards: I am a bastard begot, bastard instructed, bastard in mind, bastard in valour, in every thing illegitimate. One bear will not bite another, and wherefore should one bastard? Take heed, the quarrel's 20 most ominous to us: if the son of a whore fight for a whore, he tempts judgement: farewell, bastard.

[*Exit.*

Mar. The devil take thee, coward! [*Exit.*

SCENE VIII — *Another part of the field*

Enter HECTOR

Hect. Most putrefied core, so fair without,
Thy goodly armour thus hath cost thy life.
Now is my day's work done; I'll take good breath:
Rest, sword; thou hast thy fill of blood and death.

[*Puts off his helmet and hangs his shield behind him.*

Enter ACHILLES *and* MYRMIDONS

Achil. Look, Hector, how the sun begins to set;
How ugly night comes breathing at his heels:
Even with the vail and darking of the sun,
To close the day up, Hector's life is done.

Hect. I am unarm'd; forego this vantage, Greek.

Achil. Strike, fellows, strike; this is the man I seek. [*Hector falls.* 10
So, Ilion, fall thou next! now, Troy, sink down!
Here lies thy heart, thy sinews, and thy bone.
On, Myrmidons; and cry you all amain,
'Achilles hath the mighty Hector slain.'
[*A retreat sounded.*
Hark! a retire upon our Grecian part.

Myr. The Trojan trumpets sound the like, my lord.

Achil. The dragon wing of night o'erspreads the earth,
And stickler-like the armies separates.
My half-supp'd sword that frankly would have fed,
Pleased with this dainty bait, thus goes to bed. 20
[*Sheathes his sword.*
Come, tie his body to my horse's tail;
Along the field I will the Trojan trail.
[*Exeunt. A retreat sounded.*

SCENE IX — *Another part of the field*

Enter AGAMEMNON, AJAX, MENELAUS, NESTOR, DIOMEDES, *and the rest, marching. Shouts within*

Agam. Hark! hark! what shout is that!

Nest. Peace, drums!

[*Within*] 'Achilles! Achilles! Hector's slain! Achilles!'

Dio. The bruit is, Hector's slain, and by Achilles.

Ajax. If it be so, yet bragless let it be;
Great Hector was a man as good as he.

Agam. March patiently along: let one be sent
To pray Achilles see us at our tent.

If in his death the gods have us befriended, 10
Great Troy is ours, and our sharp wars are ended.
[*Exeunt, marching.*

SCENE X — *Another part of the field*

Enter ÆNEAS, PARIS, ANTENOR, *and* DEIPHOBUS

Æne. Stand, ho! yet are we masters of the field:
Never go home; here starve we out the night.

Enter TROILUS

Tro. Hector is slain.
All. Hector! The gods forbid!
Tro. He's dead; and at the murderer's horse's tail
In beastly sort dragg'd through the shameful field.
Frown on, you heavens, effect your rage with speed!
Sit, gods, upon your thrones, and smile at Troy!
I say, at once let your brief plagues be mercy,
And linger not our sure destructions on!
Æne. My lord, you do discomfort all the host. 10
Tro. You understand me not that tell me so:
I do not speak of flight, of fear, of death,
But dare all imminence that gods and men
Address their dangers in. Hector is gone:
Who shall tell Priam so, or Hecuba?
Let him that will a screech-owl aye be call'd,
Go in to Troy, and say there 'Hector's dead:'
There is a word will Priam turn to stone,
Make wells and Niobes of the maids and wives,
Cold statues of the youth, and, in a word, 20
Scare Troy out of itself. But march away:

Hector is dead; there is no more to say.
Stay yet. You vile abominable tents,
Thus proudly pight upon our Phrygian plains,
Let Titan rise as early as he dare,
I'll through and through you! and, thou great-
sized coward,
No space of earth shall sunder our two hates:
I'll haunt thee like a wicked conscience still,
That mouldeth goblins swift as frenzy's thoughts.
Strike a free march to Troy! with comfort go: 30
Hope of revenge shall hide our inward woe.
[*Exeunt Æneas and Trojans.*

As Troilus *is going out, enter, from the other side,* Pandarus

Pan. But hear you, hear you!

Tro. Hence, broker-lackey! ignomy and shame
Pursue thy life, and live aye with thy name! [*Exit.*

Pan. A goodly medicine for my aching bones! O world! world! world! thus is the poor agent despised! O traitors and bawds, how earnestly are you set a-work, and how ill requited! why should our endeavour be so loved and the performance so loathed? what verse for it? what 40 instance for it? Let me see:

Full merrily the humble-bee doth sing,
Till he hath lost his honey and his sting;
And being once subdued in armed tail,
Sweet honey and sweet notes together fail.

Good traders in the flesh, set this in your painted cloths:

As many as be here of Pandar's hall,
Your eyes, half out, weep out at Pandar's fall;
Or if you cannot weep, yet give some groans, 50
Though not for me, yet for your aching bones.
Brethren and sisters of the hold-door trade,
Some two months hence my will shall here be made:
It should be now, but that my fear is this,
Some galled goose of Winchester would hiss:
Till then I'll sweat and seek about for eases,
And at that time bequeath you my diseases. [*Exit.*

As many as be here of Pandar's hall,
Your eyes, half out, weep out at Pandar's fall;
Or if you cannot weep, yet give some groans, 50
Though not for me, yet for your aching bones.
Brethren and sisters of the hold-door trade,
Some two months hence my will shall here be made: 55
It should be now, but that my fear is this,
Some galled goose of Winchester would hiss.
Till then I'll sweat and seek about for eases,
And at that time bequeath you my diseases. [Exit.]

SUMMARIES AND NOTES

PROLOGUE

Because of the style of the Prologue, some scholars doubt that it is the work of Shakespeare and attribute it to Chapman or some other dramatist, a view not generally accepted. The Prologue does not appear in the Quarto.

2. ***orgulous.*** This word appears many times in Caxton's *Recuyell of the Historyes of Troye.* In the Third Book of this work, it appears four times and is used in each case with the word proud. The spellings of the word vary: "the orguyllous and proud"; "hardy orguyllous and proude"; "the orguyllous and prowde peple"; and "by our orguyell and pryde."

3. ***port of Athens.*** "the Kings and the princes of all the provynces of grece assemblid them to gyder at the porte of athens for to go to troye" (Caxton).

5. ***sixty and nine.*** "The some of Kynges and dukes that were comen thedar were sixty and nyne . . . assemblyd at the porte of Athens" (Caxton).

15. ***six-gated city.*** Troy, according to legend, had six gates in its walls. In speaking of them Caxton says, "In this Cyte were sixe pryncipall gates of whome that one was named Dardane. the second tymbria. the thirde helyas. the fourthe chetas. the fifthe troyenne and the sixthe antenorides."

23. ***prologue arm'd.*** The actor who recited the prologue was simply known by that name. He usually was dressed in a long black cloak, but in this play he was appropriately dressed in a suit of armor. In Jonson's *Poetaster* (1601), the Prologue was dressed in similar fashion, and to him this Prologue refers.

30. ***Like, or find fault.*** This expression is typical of Shakespeare's attitude toward his work. The titles of the comedies *As You Like It* and *Twelfth Night* or *What You Will* convey the same idea.

ACT I — SCENE 1

It is the eighth year of the siege of Troy. Our first glimpse of young Troilus shows him madly in love with the wanton Cressida and chafing under the yoke of war which restrains him from wooing her. He is desirous of having Pandarus intercede for him with Cressida, but Pandarus is "as tetchy to be woo'd to woo," as Cressida is "stubborn-chaste against all suit."

The division into acts and scenes, which is found in neither Folio nor Quarto except for the heading *Actus Primus: Scœna Prima* in the Folio, was first made by Rowe (ed. 1709). In fact the reader must constantly remember that many of the divisions in Shakespeare's plays were first made by Rowe who had in mind an eighteenth-century localized stage. The Elizabethan plays were given as continuously as possible with brief pauses where necessary, but with no such fixed divisions and shifts of scenes as Rowe made.

39. ***a storm.*** Rowe made this emendation. The reading of the Folio is "a-scorn," that of the Quarto, "a scorn."

49. ***Cassandra's wit.*** "Cassandra was of fayr stature and clere. Roundmouthed, wyse, shyning eyen She lovyd virginyte. And knewe moche of thynges to come by astronomye and other Sciences" (Caxton).

70. ***mends,*** "Make the best of a bad bargain," a proverbial expression of the time. It is on this proverb that Pandarus is playing. Shakespeare, like Chaucer, represents Pandarus as being fond of proverbs and saws.

80. ***as fair on Friday.*** Cressida is as attractive on a week day when she is dressed in plain clothes as Helen is on Sunday when she is dressed in her finery. This is a curious anachronism; the days of the week were not named at the time of the Greeks when the action is supposed to have taken place.

85. ***to stay behind her father.*** Cressida's father, Calchas, according to Caxton, "a great learned bishop of Troy," had been sent by Priam to consult the oracle of Delphi concerning the outcome of the war threatened by Agamemnon. When Apollo told Calchas that the Greeks were to be victorious by agreement of the gods, and urged him to desert to their army, he took the advice, leaving Cressida in Troy.

103. ***Daphne's love.*** Troilus asks Apollo's aid in the name of Daphne, a water nymph, whom Apollo had at one time loved. Daphne had resisted the sun-god and had been changed into a laurel tree by her father, a river-god.

106. ***Ilium.*** This refers to Priam's palace and not to the city. "In the most apparent place of the cyte upon a roche the Kinge Pryant dide do make hys ryche palays that was named Ylyion" (Caxton).

113. ***Æneas.*** Shakespeare follows the character of Æneas as drawn by Caxton: "Eneas had a grete body discrete mervayllously in his werkis will bespoken and attempryd in his wordes. Full of good counceyll and of science conneyng He had his visage joyouse and the eyen clere and graye. And was the richest man of troye after the Kyng pryant in townes and castellys."

SCENE 2

From Cressida's man, Alexander, we learn the gossip that Hector is angry at the fall he received in an encounter with Ajax. Pandarus, interceding with Cressida, declares Troilus a better man than Hector, and more beloved by Helen than Paris. Cressida left alone confesses that she has been "stubborn-chaste" because "men prize the things ungained."

1. ***Hecuba.*** "The quene hecuba was a rude woman and seemed better a man than a woman. She was a noble woman passinge sage debonayre And honeste and lovying the werkes of Charyte" (Caxton).

6. ***Andromache.*** "Andrometha the wyfe of Hector was a passing fayr woman and whyte and that had fayr eyen and fayr heer. She was amonge alle other women ryght honeste and attempyryd in her werkes" (Caxton).

23. ***humours.*** In Shakespeare's time, it was commonly believed that the four liquids or humours of the body were: blood, phlegm, black bile, and yellow bile. The preponderance of any of these humours supposedly determined a man's temperament and any irregularity in their proportion to one another led to disease.

30. ***Briareus,*** the fabulous giant who was supposed to have a hundred hands.

31. ***Argus,*** the mythical monster with a hundred eyes which in turn slept and watched.

175–176. ***his sons.*** Priam, according to various accounts, had from eight to fifty sons, both legitimate and illegitimate. Some authorities state that Priam's daughters are included in the total number listed as sons.

205. ***Antenor.*** "Antenor was long and lene And spakce moche But he was discrete and of grete Industrye And whom the Kynge Pryant loved gretly And gladly playd amonge his felawship And was a ryght wyse man" (Caxton).

shrewd. The reading of both Q and F is *shrow'd.*

211–213. ***give you the nod . . . the rich shall have more,*** a pun based on the word nod, meaning a simpleton, and the Biblical sentence, "To him that hath shall be given."

214. ***Hector.*** "The fyrste of the Sones was named Hector the moste worthy & beste Knyght of the world" (Caxton).

228. ***Paris.*** "The second Sone was named Parys and to surname Alixandre the whiche was the fayrest Knyght of the world, and the beste shoter and drawer of a bowe" (Caxton).

237. ***Helenus.*** "The fourthe was named Helenus a man of grete scyence And knewe all the Artes lyberall" (Caxton).

246. ***Deiphobus.*** "The thyrde was called deyphebus ryght hardy and discrite" (Caxton).

247. ***Troilus.*** "The fifth & the laste was callid Troylus that was one of the beste Knyghtes & aspre that was in his tyme" (Caxton).

267. ***Achilles.*** "Achilles was of right grete beautte blonke heeris & cryspe gray eyen and grete of Amyable sighte, large brestes & brode sholdres, grete Armes, his raynes hyghe ynowh an huygh man of grete stature and had no pareyll ne like to hym amonge alle the grekes desiryng to fighte, large in yestes And outerageous in dispense" (Caxton).

SCENE 3

In this famous debating scene, the Greek leaders argue in long philosophic discourses over the causes of their failures. Ulysses deplores the lack of unity through "neglection of degree." He and Nestor scheme to send Ajax to answer the challenge of Hector, in the hope that "Ajax employ'd plucks [will pluck] down Achilles' plumes," because the latter has become boastful and indolent.

38. ***Boreas,*** the north wind.

39. ***Thetis,*** a sea-goddess and mother of Achilles, in all probability confused by Shakespeare with Tethys, the wife of Oceanus, god of the ocean, whose name was a common synonym for the sea.

42. ***Perseus' horse.*** When Perseus went to rescue Andromeda from the sea monster, he rode Pegasus, a horse which sprang from the blood of Medusa. Pegasus was actually the property of Bellerophon.

54. ***Retorts.*** Both Q and F read *Retires.*

58. ***Ulysses.*** "Ulixes was a moste fayr man among all the grekes But he was deceyvable. And subtill. And sayd thynges Joyously. He was a right grete lyar And was so well bespoken that he had none felawe ne like to hym" (Caxton).

75–137. The aristocratic idea of government, which Ulysses expresses, had its origin in Plato's *Republic* and was almost universal during the Renaissance. (J. H. Hanford, *Studies in Philology,* 13, 100–109.)

92. ***aspects.*** The position of a planet with reference to other planets is known as its aspect. Astrologists foretell the future by studying the aspects of the stars and planets.

129. ***general's disdain'd.*** Shakespeare had sufficient knowledge of psychology to know that when a man loses his respect for a superior, his own inferiors begin to lose their respect for him.

160. ***Typhon,*** the giant with a hundred heads who attempted to overthrow Jupiter, but was defeated and imprisoned under Mount Etna.

168. ***Vulcan and his wife.*** Vulcan, who was one of the most ugly of the gods, had for his wife the beautiful Venus, the goddess of love.

174. ***gorget.*** Shakespeare portrays his characters as being dressed in the armor and clothing of his own Elizabethan period. The ancient Greeks used very little armor; so the reference to the gorget, a yoke-like defense for the throat and chest, is an anachronism.

205. ***bed-work,*** the theory of war or the planning of military measures in contrast with the practical side of carrying out or putting the theory into practice.

215. ***'fore our tent.*** When this play was presented in the Globe, Æneas entered the fore-stage from the side and appeared in front of the rear-stage which in this scene represented a tent.

230. ***youthful Phœbus.*** The sun was commonly referred to as Phœbus in poetry and plays. In the morning, the sun was considered young and therefore the morning looked coldly on him, as it did not yet know his power and heat.

262. ***long-continued truce.*** Until modern times, truces played a great part as neither side could continue steady warfare. Caxton refers to the many truces during the Trojan War, and Shakespeare has incorporated them into his play.

272. *to him this challenge.* This challenge savors of the medieval knights rather than of the ancient Greeks who as a rule thought little or nothing of their women.

316. *seeded pride . . . must be cropp'd.* When a plant or weed reaches maturity, its seed pods burst, and the seeds are cast to the four winds to scatter and grow. Achilles' pride is similar; it must be cropp'd before it can cast its seeds among the other Greek commanders.

378. *great Myrmidon,* Achilles whose Thessalian followers were called Myrmidons.

ACT II — SCENE 1

We are introduced to the scurrilous clown, Thersites, who has been sent by Ajax to learn of Hector's proclamation. He successively rails at both Ajax and Achilles, and vituperatively belittles the wit of the beefy pair.

14. *mongrel.* The father of Ajax, according to Caxton, was Telamon, a Greek, who had carried off Hesione, a sister of Priam, who became the mother of Ajax. He was, therefore, half Greek and half Trojan.

37. *Cerberus,* the three-headed dog which guarded the gates of Hades.

Proserpina, wife of Pluto and queen of Hades.

SCENE 2

The Greeks promise to raise the siege if Helen is returned, and a war indemnity is paid to them. The Trojans reject the offer. In a long dialogue, we learn that although Hector has issued the challenge, he prefers peace and wishes Helen to be returned. Paris and Troilus, however, are convinced that peace would not be worth the loss of glory and honor involved. The entrance of the raving Cassandra presages the ultimate defeat of the Trojans.

77. *old aunt.* Hesione, a sister of King Priam, was carried off to Greece by Hercules who had rescued her from great danger and had been refused his promised reward. He gave her to his friend, Telamon. Priam, angered by this, proposed an expedition against the Greeks to recover her. Paris, who had been promised the fairest wife in Greece by Venus, offered to lead the expedition which would either recover

Hesione or else bring back a Greek queen as a captive to atone for the ravishment of Priam's sister. The offer of Paris was accepted; he went to Greece where he took advantage of the hospitality of Menelaus to carry off his wife, Helen. The result was the Trojan War. (See note, ii. 1. 14.)

82. ***launch'd above a thousand ships.*** Shakespeare evidently based this line on those in Marlowe's *Doctor Faustus*, "Was this the face that launch'd a thousand ships, And burnt the topless towers of Ilium" (Sc. xiv. 83).

101. ***Cry, Trojans, cry!*** Cassandra, according to Caxton, foretold evil both before and after the expedition of Paris.

110. ***firebrand brother.*** Before the birth of Paris, his mother, Hecuba, dreamed that she would give birth to a firebrand which would destroy Troy. Paris was exposed on a mountain to die, but a shepherd found and adopted him.

166. ***Aristotle,*** a Greek philosopher (348 to 322 B.C.), and a tutor of Alexander the Great, of Macedonia. In Aristotle's *Nicomachean Ethics,* there is a statement that young men are not fit to study *political* philosophy. Shakespeare makes Aristotle say that they are unfit to hear *moral* philosophy. Followers of the Baconian theory, who believe that the plays now credited to Shakespeare were the work of Francis Bacon (1561–1626), have placed great importance on this substitution of the word *moral* for the word *political.* They declare that Bacon made the same mistake in his *Advancement of Learning.* Sir Sidney Lee has shown, however, that this interpretation of Aristotle's words was usual during the sixteenth and seventeenth centuries.

SCENE 3

The jester, Thersites, rails again at Achilles (who has "inveighed" the clown from Ajax) and calls all the Greek leaders "fools." Achilles is appointed to meet Hector but sulks in his tent, and refuses. Agamemnon believes Ajax should persuade Achilles to fight, but Ulysses and Nestor see to it that Ajax is appointed in his stead.

27. ***slipped out.*** A slip was a counterfeit coin made of brass and covered with silver.

43. ***cheese.*** It was a common belief that eating cheese aided one's digestion.

111. ***elephant.*** The Elizabethans, to whom the elephant was a myth or at least an unknown animal of the far East, believed that the elephant had no joints.

185. ***death-tokens.*** Certain spots which appeared on those suffering from the plague were supposed to be signs of approaching death. The great London plagues of 1593 and 1603 caused thousands of deaths and kept the people in constant fear.

204. ***Cancer.*** The sun, "great Hyperion," enters the sign of Cancer, the Crab, in the zodiac, on June 21, at the season of the summer solstice.

231. ***A' would have ten shares.*** The phrase "ten shares" is thought by some critics to refer to the ten shares of stock in the Globe Theatre of which Shakespeare held one. As Will Kemp, the comedian, was dissatisfied with his share of the stock, Shakespeare may be comparing Ajax to Kemp.

258. ***Milo.*** This famous athlete of Crotona won renown by carrying a bull on his shoulders through the stadium of Olympia. The incident is described in Cicero's *De Senectute.* This is another anachronism, as Milo lived in the sixth century B.C., long after the Trojan War.

ACT III — SCENE 1

Composed principally of small talk and repartee, this scene reveals Helen, like Cressida, another practiced coquette. Pandarus comes to ask Helen to make excuse to King Priam for Troilus who is supping with Cressida.

16. ***Grace.*** In England a duke or an archbishop by the rules of etiquette is addressed as "Your Grace."

SCENE 2

Pandarus, as he has promised, brings Troilus and Cressida together. In this, their first love scene, we see how ably the clever Cressida has brought Troilus under her spell. They profess undying love for each other. Pandarus with characteristic innuendo leaves them together for the night.

10. ***Stygian banks,*** banks of the river Styx.

11. ***Charon,*** the ferryman who rowed souls across the river Styx to Hades.

17. ***here i' the orchard.*** As stage settings in Shakespeare's day were limited, the playwright included in his lines references to the setting of the scene. This expression is merely a hint to the audience that the place is an orchard, *i.e.* a garden.

48. ***draw this curtain.*** Pictures, until a score of years ago, were covered with a curtain to protect them from dirt and light. In this case, the expression simply means "remove your veil."

51. ***rub on, and kiss the mistress,*** a pun based on the game of bowling in which the jack was sometimes called mistress. The expression means, "overcome all obstacles and reach the goal."

52. ***fee-farm,*** a grant of land in perpetuity for which a small rent or fee was collected.

139. ***Cunning.*** Greg and Alexander believe that the original reading *Comming* of both Q and F should be retained.

216–217. ***press it to death.*** During the Middle Ages, certain criminals who refused to plead guilty were pressed to death. The criminal was staked out on the floor, a heavy plate was placed on his chest, and heavy stones were placed on the plate until the man either confessed or died. There is a description of a torture chamber and of a man being pressed to death in Victor Hugo's novel, *The Laughing Man.*

SCENE 3

Calchas (note i. 1. 83), who has "incurred a traitor's name," asks the Greeks to pay him for his services by agreeing to exchange Cressida for a Trojan captive, Antenor. When the discussion ends, the Greek leaders purposely snub Achilles, and Ulysses delivers to him a sermon on the diminishing of fame by the passage of time. Achilles, we learn, is in love with Polyxena, Priam's daughter. The scene ends with the sending of an invitation to Hector to come unarmed to Achilles' tent.

4. ***"Through the sight I bear in things to love."*** This line has caused much trouble. Alexander believes the line should read *things to come* referring to Calchas' gift of prophecy; Haworth asserts, on the unsubstantial basis of Halliwell-Phillipps' reduced facsimile of the First Folio, that the word should be *fight* — but in the original folio as well as in the full-sized facsimiles the word is clearly *sight.* Assuming *fight* as the reading, he interprets the line "Through the struggle I endure in giving up things, dear to me," but the usual interpretation is "Through my peculiar insight into what is desirable." (*Times* Literary Supplement, May 21, 1925.)

95. ***A strange fellow here.*** Plato (427–346 B.C.), the Greek philosopher, is probably the "strange fellow" since the lines which Ulysses quotes resemble a passage in Plato's dialogue, "*First Alcibiades.*"

178. ***give.*** Both Q and F read *goe.*

194. ***one of Priam's daughters.*** According to Caxton, Achilles, who was in love with Polyxena, had obtained permission to marry her from her parents King Priam and Queen Hecuba, on the condition that he bring about peace between the Greeks and the Trojans. His efforts failed; so he shut himself up in his tent in melancholy. After the death of Patroclus, Achilles took the field and slew Hector. Hecuba lured Achilles to the Temple of Apollo to discuss his marriage with Polyxena, and there had Paris slay him treacherously to avenge the death of Hector. At the end of the war, the Greeks were delayed by unfavorable winds until, at the insistence of Calchas, they sacrificed Polyxena to atone for the murder of Achilles by her brother, Paris. According to Caxton, Achilles did not fall in love with Polyxena until after the death of Hector, but Shakespeare for purposes of plot makes the change.

197. ***Plutus,*** the god of wealth, not to be confounded with Pluto, god of the underworld.

209. ***Pyrrhus,*** the young son of Achilles, who, according to Caxton, slew the Amazon queen, Penthesilea, Hecuba, and Polyxena.

215. ***The fool slides o'er the ice.*** There was an anecdote current in Shakespeare's company, probably told to Shakespeare by Robert Armin (1599–1603), a fellow member, that a half-witted, stage-struck country-fellow attempted to follow a company of players, and passed safely over an expanse of ice so thin that a brickbat dropped on it broke through. (Halliwell-Phillipps, *A Nest of Ninies* [1605–1608], Shakespeare Society, 1842, pp. 37, 38.)

There are several interpretations of the passage in the play possible. One is, "You (Achilles) should break the thin ice Ajax is sliding over, and so keep him in his own place" (Tatlock). Another is, "The fool (Ajax) can run risks which would be fatal to, or unworthy of, a man of your (Achilles') dignity and position" (Paradise).

ACT IV — SCENE 1

After a spirited interchange between Diomedes and Æneas, the former delivers Antenor to the Trojans. Paris in asking, "Who, in your thoughts, deserves fair Helen best, Myself or Menelaus?" occasions Diomedes' denunciation of her as a wanton.

23. ***Anchises,*** the father of Æneas.

24. ***Venus,*** the mother of Æneas.

SCENE 2

It is early morning. Troilus and Cressida, extremely happy, part in a most appealing love scene. Pandarus greets them with good-morning ribaldry. Æneas arrives and informs them of the fate decided for Cressida. She declares that she has forgotten her father and "will not go from Troy."

32. ***capocchia;*** in both Q and F *chipochia.*

SCENE 3

Troilus promises Paris to deliver Cressida to Diomedes.

SCENE 4

The love of Troilus and Cressida is disturbed by feelings of jealousy and distrust as Troilus insistently cautions Cressida to be faithful. They promise constancy to each other, and exchange a glove and a sleeve as tokens of faithfulness. Diomedes leads away Cressida.

28. ***Have the gods envy?*** The ancients believed that great beauty, happiness, skill, or strength made the gods envious, and so led to misfortune.

122. ***zeal.*** Both Q and F read *seale.*

SCENE 5

When Diomedes leads Cressida into the lists at the Greek camp, the leaders roundly salute her with kisses while she engages with them in coarse repartee. After she has departed, Ulysses condemns her as a "wanton."

As Ajax and Hector enter the lists, Ulysses voices the opinion of Æneas that Troilus is a better warrior than Hector. A few blows are exchanged between Ajax and Hector, but the latter refuses to continue the struggle because of his kinship with Ajax. Hector is introduced to the Greek leaders as a friend but is quite rudely received, especially by Achilles. After bragging of their prowess, Hector and Achilles agree to fight on the morrow. The scene ends with Ulysses agreeing to lead Troilus to Cressida.

9. ***Aquilon,*** the north wind.

62. ***sluttish spoils of opportunity,*** women of loose morals; prostitutes.

141. ***Neoptolemus,*** apparently another name for Achilles, though eminent authorities have disagreed as to just whom Shakespeare meant. Pyrrhus, the son of Achilles, was called Neoptolemus, but at this time he was a boy and "still at home" (iii. 3. 209).

142. ***Oyes.*** Both Q and F read *O yes.*

ACT V — SCENE 1

A token, sent from Polyxena by Thersites to Achilles, reminds him of the oath he made her to fail the Greeks. Thersites rails against the devotion of Achilles for Patroclus. After Hector is led to his sleeping-quarters, Ulysses and Troilus follow Diomedes to Cressida's tent; Thersites in a soliloquy presents Diomedes as a false rogue, and Cressida as his drab.

20. ***rotten diseases of the south.*** Diseases were supposed to be borne by the south wind.

55–56. ***goodly transformation of Jupiter.*** Jupiter turned himself into a white bull in order to win or abduct Europa.

SCENE 2

Ulysses and Troilus, before Calchas' tent, spy on the love scene between Cressida and Diomedes. Cressida gives Diomedes the sleeve Troilus had given her as a token of constancy. Troilus is completely disillusioned and swears to have Diomedes' life. Thersites, the interpreter and commentator, sums up the whole controversy as consisting merely of "wars and lechery."

56. ***potato-finger.*** Potatoes were supposed to have the power of stimulating sexual desires.

151. ***Ariachne's broken woof.*** Ariachne's skill in weaving angered the goddess Pallas, who turned her into a spider.

SCENE 3

Back in Troy Hector is determined to fight in spite of the warning of Andromache, Cassandra, and Priam that the day is ominous. Pandarus brings a letter to Troilus from Cressida, which he promptly tears to bits.

38. ***fits a lion.*** The lion was supposed to be very merciful as in the fable of the lion and the mouse, familiar to all school children. The idea is not new; Pliny in his *Natural History* declares, "The lion alone of all wild beasts is gentle to those that humble themselves before him, and will not touch any such upon their submission, but spareth what creature soever lieth prostrate before him."

SCENE 4

This scene again presents Thersites scurrilously analyzing the situation. He is interrupted first by the fight of Diomedes and Troilus, and then by Hector who is looking for a noble Greek to kill.

At the Globe Theatre in Shakespeare's day, most of these scenes of battle were virtually one.

SCENE 5

Diomedes dispatches a servant to Cressida with Troilus' horse and the false message that he, Diomedes, has "chastised the amorous Trojan." Agamemnon enters with the news that the battle is going against the Greeks. Achilles and Ajax are awakened out of their indolence; Achilles, because Patroclus is slain; Ajax, because a friend has been slain. Achilles declares that he will meet none but Hector; Ajax, none but Troilus.

6. ***Polydamas,*** the son of Antenor.

7. ***Menon,*** the cousin of Achilles.

Margarelon, a son of Priam.

8. ***Doreus,*** an earl accompanying Ajax.

11. ***Epistrophus,*** an ally of the Greeks.

Cedius, a brother of Epistrophus. *Epistrophus* and *Cedius;* spelled in both Q and F, and also in Caxton *Epistropus* and *Cedus.*

Polyxenes, a Greek duke who was slain by Hector.

12. ***Amphimachus,*** "kyng of Calydone," was slain by Æneas.

12. ***Thoas,*** a king and cousin of Achilles.

13. ***Palamedes,*** a Greek duke who was slain by Paris with a poisoned arrow.

14. ***Sagittary.*** "A mervayllous beste that was called *sagittayre,* that behinde the myddes was an horse, and to fore a man: this beste was heery like an horse, and had his eyen rede as a cole, and shotte well with a bowe: this beste made the Greeks sore aferde, and slew many of them with his bowe" (Caxton). Diomedes is credited with killing the monster.

SCENE 6

Troilus is fighting both Diomedes and Ajax. Achilles meets Hector but refuses to fight, and offers the excuse that his "arms are out of use." Troilus enters declaring that although Ajax has taken Æneas, he will prevent Ajax from carrying him off.

SCENE 7

Achilles instructs his Myrmidons how to murder Hector. Thersites proclaims that "the cuckold and the cuckold-maker" (Menelaus and Paris) are engaged.

SCENE 8

Wearied by fighting, Hector removes his helmet and shield. Achilles and the Myrmidons kill him from behind.

18. ***stickler-like.*** An umpire at a duel was called a stickler. His duty was to part the duelists with his staff if the issue could be decided without bloodshed.

21. ***tie his body.*** Shakespeare has arranged this scene as told by Caxton. Caxton says of the Greeks' treatment of the body of Troilus, "Achilles . . . toke the body and bonde hit to the taylle of his horse And so drewe hit after hym thrugh oute the ooste." Shakespeare portrays the Greeks as treating the body of Hector in that fashion. Caxton declares that the body of Hector was brought back to Troy and that the body of Troilus was buried during a truce accorded by the Greeks.

SCENE 9

The soldiers announce Hector's death to the Greek leaders.

SCENE 10

Troilus announces Hector's death to the Trojan leaders, and pictures his body as being dragged ignominiously around the field tied to the tail of Achilles' horse. The drama ends with an epilogue full of obscene and localized Elizabethan wit delivered by Pandarus to the audience.

19. *Niobes.* Niobe, the daughter of Tantalus, and wife of Aurphion, king of Thebes. Her seven sons and daughters were slain by Apollo and Artemis.

46–47. *painted cloths,* wall coverings in Elizabethan houses, decorated with water-color pictures, often with mottoes and maxims painted as if proceeding from the mouths of the figures.

APPENDIX A

DRAMATIS PERSONÆ

None of the Folios has a list of characters. It is first given by Rowe (1709).

The following biographical accounts are adapted from Smith's *Dictionary of Greek and Roman Biography and Mythology*. Under (*a*) is given the Homeric version, under (*b*) the version as developed by the Middle Ages and subsequently refashioned by Shakespeare. The following chart has been included so that the reader may have before him for consultation a panorama of this development from Homer to Shakespeare.

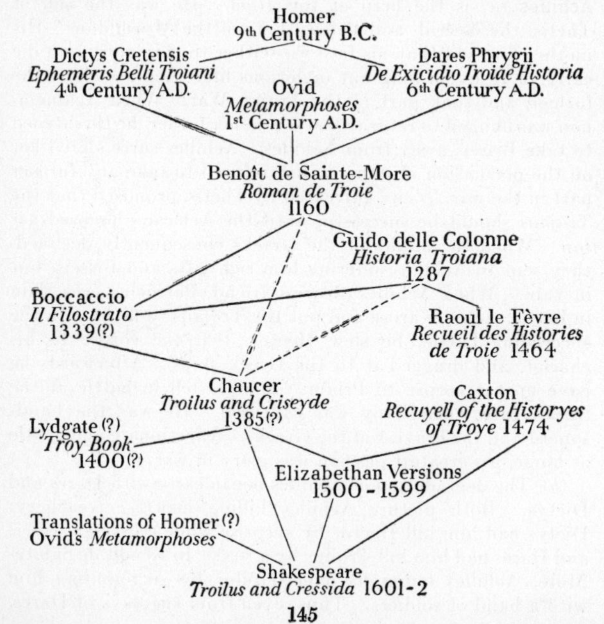

The medieval Troy story is seen to arise out of the Homeric fictions of Dictys and Dares. The elaboration of the story into a French medieval romance, in which are involved the faithful love of Troilus and the faithlessness of Cressida, is the work of Benoît de Sainte-More. Guido delle Colonne by making a Latin version of Benoît's French poem gave the romance a wide circulation. Boccaccio, who consulted both Benoît and Guido, wrought out a single and unified love story and added the character of Pandarus. Chaucer turned Boccaccio's Pandarus from an accommodating friend and gentleman into a middle-aged uncle, and Boccaccio's fickle beauty, Griseda, into the faithless yet piteous Criseyde. Shakespeare's play follows more closely Caxton's version, which harks back to Benoît, through Raoul le Fèvre and Guido, but his characterizations are in accord with Elizabethan rather than with either Homeric or Chaucerian conceptions.

Achilles (*a*) is the hero of the *Iliad.* He was the son of Thetis, the Nereid, and Peleus, king of the Myrmidons. His mother foretold that his fate was either to gain glory and die early, or to live a long but inglorious life. Achilles chose the former, and took part in the Trojan War. When Agamemnon was obliged to return Chryseis to her father, he threatened to take Briseis away from Achilles. Achilles surrendered her on the persuasion of Athena, but refused to take any further part in the war. Zeus, entreated by Thetis, promised that the Trojans should be successful until the Achæans honored her son. When the affairs of the Greeks consequently declined, they sent to Achilles, offering him rich gifts and Briseis, but in vain. When Achilles' dearest friend, Patroclus, was slain in battle, Achilles arose and put the Trojans to flight. In the succeeding battle, he slew Hector, tied the corpse to his chariot, and dragged it to the Greek ships. Afterwards he gave up the corpse to Priam. Achilles fell in battle at the Scæan gate when Troy was captured. He was the handsomest and the bravest of the Greeks. Affectionate and gentle at home, his greatest passion was glory in war.

(*b*) The degradation of Achilles began early with Dares and Dictys. Both picture Achilles killing men by treachery: Dictys had him kill Hector by surprise while crossing a river, and Dares had him kill Troilus by a ruse. In Benoît de Sainte-More, Achilles triumphs over Troilus by surrounding him with a band of soldiers. Thus, even from the days of Dares,

Achilles was ready for Shakespeare's drawing; a braggart, a traitor, and a coward — a slacker, for the sake of Priam's daughter.

Æneas (*a*), Trojan hero in the Homeric story, was the son of Anchises and Aphrodite, and was born on Mount Ida. He took no part in the Trojan War until after Achilles had attacked him and driven away his flocks. Then he gathered his Dardanians and became one of the Trojan leaders. LATER STORIES. — Most accounts agree that after the capture of Troy, Æneas withdrew to Mount Ida; and that from there he crossed over to Europe, finally settling in Italy, where he became the ancestral hero of the Romans. Vergil's *Æneid* gives an account of his wanderings on the way, and of his love affair with Dido at Carthage.

(*b*) The partiality of the English for the Trojans is in perfect harmony with a Latin tradition, transmitted from antiquity through the Middle Ages to the Renaissance. Latin rather than Greek literature made up the classical education of the Middle Ages and of the greater part of the Renaissance. Because of Vergil's *Æneid* the Romans believed themselves descendants of the Trojans through Æneas. The barbarians who overran Rome came also to consider themselves related to this great tradition which grew and spread until the Trojans became the parent nation for the new European states including also the British Isles founded by Brute, the descendant of Æneas. Both Dares and Dictys represent Antenor and Æneas as secretly delivering the city into the hands of the Greeks, and Dares alone says it is they, and not the Homeric Sinon, who gave the signal for the return of the Greek fleet to Troy. Shakespeare, however, depicts Æneas as honorable and patriotic, though pompous and boastful in delivering Hector's challenge.

Agamemnon (*a*), called by Homer the son of Atreus, was brought up together with Ægisthus, son of Thyestes, in the house of Atreus. After the murder of Atreus by Ægisthus and Thyestes, Agamemnon and Menelaus went to Sparta. Here Agamemnon married Clytemnestra, daughter of King Tyndareos, became king of Mycenæ and the most powerful prince in Greece. He was chosen commander-in-chief of the Greek forces that gathered at Aulis to sail for Troy in order to recover Helen, wife of his brother, who had eloped with Paris. At Aulis, Agamemnon killed a stag sacred to Artemis, who thereupon visited the Greek army with a pestilence, and produced a calm which prevented the Greeks from leaving the port. To appease her wrath, Agamemnon consented to sacrifice his daughter Iphigenia. The calm ceased, and the army sailed to Troy. In the tenth year of the war Agamemnon quarreled with Achilles over the Trojan maidens, Cryseis and Bryseis. When Troy fell, Agamemnon received Cassandra, Priam's daughter, as his prize. On his return home he was murdered by Ægisthus, who had become the paramour of Clytemnestra in her husband's absence.

(*b*) Agamemnon's only contribution to the action of the play is his grant of Calchas' request to exchange Antenor with the Trojans for Cressida. As the commander-in-chief of the Greek forces, he has suffered a come-down in Shakespeare almost to the point of being a nonentity. His character, one of an empty haughtiness, is taken off by Thersites: "Here's Agamemnon, an honest fellow enough, and one that loves quails; but he has not so much brain as ear-wax." (v. 1. 53–55.)

Ajax (*a*), called Aias by the Greeks, was the son of Telamon, king of Salamis, and grandson of Æacus. He sailed against Troy with twelve ships. Answering with other chieftains Hector's challenge, he received the lot to fight, and wounded Hector. Ajax was also one of the ambassadors sent to conciliate Achilles. In the contest over the armor of Achilles, he was conquered by Ulysses, a defeat, says Homer, which caused his death. Another version relates that he went mad over his defeat, rushed out and slaughtered the sheep of the Greek army, and committed suicide.

(*b*) Ajax as a partly comic figure in Shakespeare is amply accounted for in later Greek, Latin, and medieval literature. Through the *Iliad* and the *Odyssey* he retains his heroic dignity, but in Sophocles, though still dignified, he is an example of insolent impiety, showing hatred, revenge, and braggadocio towards the gods. Ovid's account makes him still meaner and more arrogant, almost a lily-livered boaster, without intelligence. He kills himself saying that none but Ajax can conquer Ajax. This is the Ajax that was known to the Elizabethans, and his classical savagery and mad absurdity they eagerly seized upon and greatly developed. In Shakespeare he becomes a comic paradox, a combination of the Ajax of Homer and the Elizabethan Ajax, a beefy, absurd egotist, and yet a mighty warrior.

Andromache (*a*) was the daughter of Eetion, king of Cilician Thebes. She was married to Hector, by whom she had a son, Scamandrius (Astyanax). At the taking of Troy, her son was hurled from its walls, and she herself became the prize of Neoptolemus, son of Achilles, who took her to Epirus. Afterwards she married Helenus, a brother of Hector and ruler of Chaonia. After Helenus' death she followed her son, Pergamus, to Asia and died there.

(*b*) Medieval romancers are responsible for the story of Andromache's dream and her warning to Hector. For example, in Benoît de Sainte-More the scene is 271 lines in length, and Andromache is represented as bawling, beating her breast, and tearing her hair when her warning to Hector goes unheeded. The scene of farewell in Homer, however, is one of the most beautiful and moving in all poetry. Andromache's complaint is untinged by weakness or emotion; and Hector treats her with the deepest tenderness. How different from Shakespeare's Andromache, who wheedles, and his Hector, who says:

> "You train me to offend you; get you in:
> By all the everlasting gods, I'll go!"

Calchas (*a*), son of Thestor of Megara, was the wisest soothsayer among the Greeks at Troy. He foretold the duration of the Trojan War and explained the cause of Apollo's anger.

(*b*) Shakespeare's Calchas bears little resemblance to Homer's. Instead, he is fashioned after Dares, who represents him as a Trojan gone over to the Greeks in consequence of his prophetic spirit, by which he foreknew the fatal future of Troy. In Shakespeare we see him in the Greek camp while his daughter remains at Troy.

Cassandra was the daughter of Priam and Hecuba, and twin sister of Helenus. Apollo, affected by her great beauty, endowed her with the gift of prophecy upon her promise to comply with his desires; but, upon receiving the prophetic art, she broke her promise. Thereupon Apollo ordained that her prophecies should not be believed. In the Trojan War she continually foretells the impending calamities, but no one heeds her; even Priam himself thinks her mad. On the capture of Troy, she fled into the sanctuary of Athena, but was torn away from the temple and fell to the lot of Agamemnon, who took her home to Mycenæ. Here she was killed by Clytemnestra, Agamemnon's wife.

Cressida. Although the Homeric origin of the name "Cressida" may be sought in either Briseis or Chryseis, over whom Agamemnon and Achilles quarrelled, both of these characters of the *Iliad* remain throughout antiquity as Homer fashioned them. Shakespeare's coquette has another origin. The Troilus and Cressida theme was apparently invented by Benoît de Sainte-More in his *Roman de Troie*. The heroine Briseida has already the essential characteristics of Shakespeare's Cressida, for she is very comely, has a "quick and ready wit," "a *changeable* heart," and is already a faithless coquette. Although Benoît found a translator in Guido, and Guido found many imitators, it was not until Boccaccio wrote his *Filostrato* that the love story was further developed, mainly from Guido's book. The work is too profoundly subjective for the principal interest to be in Briseida, and as a consequence she becomes, though charming and voluptuous, shadowy and inconsistent. Chaucer's *Troilus* and *Criseyde* (1385?), based mainly upon Boccaccio, retains Criseyde as a widow (as in Boccaccio), but she is even more obdurate than the Italian heroine, and so complex that critics are unable to agree in estimating her character. Certainly, she receives a sympathetic treatment from Chaucer, and although the poet himself seems amazed at her treachery, he pities her, but still condemns her. Robert Henryson in the *Testament of Cressid* is responsible for Cressida's degeneration into a harlot. He drags her deeply into the mire and depicts her deserted by Diomedes, stricken by leprosy, and dying of a broken heart. An increasing morality continued to condemn her even more severely, until in the sixteenth century she became the leprous wanton of street ballads,[1] and her name a byword for a loose and faithless woman. Tradition had cast her character firmly and unalterably before Shakespeare touched her. Sympathetic treatment of her was impossible, and a chaste Cressida, such as Dryden later created, would have been jeered off the stage. It should be observed, however, that, as Rollins points out, Shakespeare's treatment of Cressida is more tolerant than that of his age; if he does not make us pity her, he does not draw her as a creature of the gutters and the stews.

[1] H. E. Rollins, P.M.L.A., Vol. 32, pp. 393–394.

Deiphobus, a son of Priam and Hecuba, was, next to Hector, the bravest among the Trojans. According to one tradition he was slain and mangled by Menelaus on the capture of Troy by the Greeks.

Diomedes (*a*), son of Tydeus and Deipyle, in the Homeric story went to Troy with eighty ships, and, next to Achilles, was the bravest Greek hero. Under Athena's protection he fought against the most distinguished Trojans such as Hector and Æneas. The *Iliad* describes him as brave in war, wise in counsel, and strong like a god.

(*b*) Benoît de Sainte-More, in order to provide a contrast to the spiritual devotion of Troilus and a motive for the inconstancy of Briseis (Cressida), transformed the honest and wise Diomedes of Homer into an arch-seducer. Chaucer's Diomedes, too, was a faithless philanderer. In the *Testament of Cressid*, Henryson, though changing the character of Cressida, retains the same Diomedes, who soon tires of his mistress and turns her out. Thus Diomedes comes to Shakespeare; though not the sneaky seducer of Benoît, he is still sensual and brutal.

Hector (*a*), chief hero of the Trojans, the eldest son of Priam and Hecuba, was the husband of Andromache, and father of Scamandrius. When Diomedes was pressing the Trojans, Hector sent a challenge for a single combat to the bravest of the Greeks; Ajax accepted. In the contest Hector was wounded, but later he repelled Ajax, fired the Greek ships, and slew Patroclus, Achilles' friend. The other Trojans fled before the wrath of Achilles into the city, but Hector remained without the walls. When he saw Achilles, however, he fled thrice around the city before he fell pierced by Achilles' spear.

(*b*) Of all the Trojan heroes in Shakespeare's play, Hector is the least caricatured. The Homeric tradition, even in medieval romances, had preserved him his nobility, and when we see him in Shakespeare as prudent and brave, with a peculiarly high sense of justice and honor, it is only because throughout the Middle Ages, and hence in Caxton's *History*, Hector played a glorious part, and Achilles an ignoble one. His Homeric character, however, though not degraded, has been slightly changed. With Shakespeare he has become a nationalist as well as a warrior. Had his good sense prevailed,

Helen would have been sent back to Menelaus, and the useless war been brought to an end.

Helen (*a*) was a daughter of Zeus and Leda, and sister of Polydeuces (Pollux) and Castor; some traditions called her a daughter of Zeus and Nemesis. Of surpassing beauty, she was wooed by the noblest chiefs of Greece; she wedded Menelaus and bore him a daughter, Hermione. She was subsequently seduced by Paris and carried to Troy. After the capture of Troy, she became reconciled to Menelaus, and returned home with him to Sparta.

(*b*) According to the *Odyssey* Helen was to transcend mortal death and be conducted to Elysium by the gods, but in Shakespeare she is of the commonest clay. In the play she speaks but thirty lines of amorous repartee with Pandarus. "Let thy song be love," she says to Pandarus; "this love will undo us all. O Cupid, Cupid, Cupid!" But Thersites sees it with a harsher reality, "Nothing but lechery! All incontinent varlets!"

Helenus, son of Priam and Hecuba, was celebrated for his prophetic powers. After the fall of Troy he foretold to Pyrrhus the suffering which awaited the Greeks who returned home by sea, and prevailed upon him to return to Epirus by land. After Pyrrhus' death he received a portion of that country, and married Andromache.

Menelaus (*a*), son of Atreus, and younger brother of Agamemnon, was king of Lacedæmon, and husband of Helen. After the Trojan War Helen became reconciled to her husband, and together with Nestor they sailed away from Troy. They wandered for eight years before reaching home. Afterwards Menelaus and Helen lived at Sparta in peace and wealth. In the Homeric poems, though he is described as reticent, his speeches are always impressive. He was brave and courageous, milder than Agamemnon, but intelligent and hospitable.

(*b*) The highly wronged Menelaus of Homer, by the time he reaches Shakespeare, has become "that shabbiest of Elizabethan butts, a cuckold." He speaks but twelve lines. To his frigid "How do you?" Achilles, offended and outraged, replies, "What, does the cuckold scorn me?" and Thersites sums up the contention with his sardonic fling, "All the argument is a cuckold and a whore."

Nestor (*a*), king of Pylos, was the only one of twelve sons not slain by Hercules. In his youth, Nestor was a distinguished warrior. At Troy he took part in all important events, both in council and battle. Through him, Agamemnon became reconciled with Achilles, and henceforth always applied to Nestor for advice. His most striking features, according to Homer, were his wisdom, justice, bravery, and eloquence.

(*b*) Though Thersites brands Nestor as "a stale old mouse-eaten dry cheese," the old man in Shakespeare's version is not a wholly disagreeable person, and retains some of his Homeric sagacity.

Pandarus. There are two persons named Pandarus in Homer, and one in Vergil, but the name is all they have in common with that character in Shakespeare. Boccaccio in his *Filostrato* was the first to add Pandarus to the Troilus and Cressida story, but his Pandaro is almost diametrically opposed in character to the Pandarus of Shakespeare. It is evident from Chaucer's *Troilus and Criseyde* that for the English the man's trade is a vile one, but for Boccaccio and the Italians this go-between is a knight who is himself in love, a faithful friend, who holds it his duty by friendship and chivalry to serve Troilus in his love affair, and who expects no reward in return.

In Chaucer's poem right and wrong hinge on medieval convention in which "honor" is the keynote. If Criseyde's "honor" is not to be stained, the preservation of absolute secrecy is necessary. Thus Pandarus, in assuming the rôle of a go-between, is taking a chance of being involved in a scandal that will besmirch both his good name and Criseyde's as well. Though he is unmoral, he is no base mercenary procurer, but rather a kindly, sympathetic friend.

Early in the sixteenth century, however, "Pander" had become a common noun, a generic name for procurer, and Shakespeare could no more raise Pandarus to respectability than he could Cressida.

Paris (*a*), also called Alexander, was the second son of Priam and Hecuba. Before his birth, Hecuba dreamed that he would bring about the ruin of his native city. Accordingly, he was exposed on Mount Ida at birth and brought up by a shepherd who gave him the name of Paris. When grown, he discovered his real origin and was received by Priam as his son. He married Œnone, daughter of the river god Cebrenis, but deserted her for Helen. The tale runs that Hera, Aphrodite, and Athena each claimed the famous golden apple, inscribed "To the fairest," for herself. Zeus ordered the decision to be entrusted to Paris. As Aphrodite promised him the fairest of women for his wife, he decided in her favor. This judgment incurred in Hera and Athena fierce hatred against Troy. Under Aphrodite's protection, Paris went to Greece, and was received at Menelaus' palace. Here he carried off Helen, Menelaus' wife. Her former suitors, the noblest chiefs of Greece, resolved to avenge her abduction and sailed against Troy. Before the walls of Troy, Paris was defeated in combat by Menelaus. On the capture of Troy, Paris was wounded by Philoctetes, returned to his wife Œnone, on Mount Ida, and died there.

(*b*) Although in general the Middle Ages dimmed the lustre of the heroes, Paris appears as one of the bravest of the Trojan warriors. In Shakespeare Paris's glory is dimmed by his refusal to follow Hector's counsel and return Helen, and by his indulging in low bantering with Pandarus.

Patroclus (*a*), while a boy, involuntarily committed murder during a dice game. He was taken by his father to Peleus at Phthia, where he met Achilles, a kinsman, and a strong friendship arose between them. He accompanied Achilles to Troy, but when his friend withdrew from battle, Patroclus followed his example. When the Greeks were hard pressed by the Trojans, he dressed in Achilles' armor and led the Myrmidons into battle. He drove back the Trojans, extinguished the fire raging among the ships, and thrice made an assault on the walls of Troy. Suddenly he was struck senseless by Apollo. Then Euphorbus ran him through, and Hector finished him with a fatal blow. After a struggle, the Greeks secured his body, and Achilles on viewing it vowed to avenge his death.

(*b*) The attachment of Patroclus to Achilles was the object of Middle Age mud-slinging. With Shakespeare he becomes a pervert and a weakling, but this degradation made it possible for Shakespeare to use him as one of the comic personages of the play.

Priam (*a*), king of Troy, was first married to Arisba, and afterwards to Hecuba. According to Homer he was the father of fifty sons, nineteen of whom were children of Hecuba. When the Greeks landed on the Trojan coast, Priam was advanced in years and took no active part in battle. According to Homer, after the death of Hector, Priam went to the tent of Achilles to ransom his son's body for burial, and obtained it. Upon the capture of Troy, he was slain by Pyrrhus, son of Achilles, at the altar of Zeus where he had taken refuge with Hecuba and her daughters.

(*b*) In *Troilus and Cressida* Priam speaks only twenty lines; Shakespeare makes no divergences from Homer's portrait of him.

Thersites (*a*), a son of Agrius, was the ugliest and most impudent talker among the Greeks at Troy. Once, when he had spoken in the assembly in an unbecoming manner against Agamemnon, he was chastised by Ulysses. Finally, he dared to revile Achilles, who in anger slew him.

(*b*) Although Shakespeare's scurrilous Thersites resembles the reviling braggart of that name in Homer, it is not likely, as most critics have asserted, that Shakespeare borrowed his Thersites directly from Chapman's *Iliad*. "Instead," as Rollins [1] points out, "he must have been chiefly influenced by Heywood's *Iron Age* or by an older play which they both used. Perhaps he knew John Heywood's (?) interlude of *Thersites*, which was printed by Tyndale, 1552–1563. . . ." Shakespeare also knew the Thersites in Arthur Golding's translation of Ovid's *Metamorphoses* (1567). Shakespeare's Thersites, like his Pandar, was intended to be purely a comic figure. Besides acting as a sort of court fool, he fulfils, in part at least, the function of Chorus in the play. In his gross and obscene language are observations of great shrewdness and significance.

Troilus (*a*), who is merely mentioned in Homer as a young and brave warrior, was a son of Priam and Hecuba, or, according to others, a son of Apollo. He fell by the hand of Achilles.

(*b*) Troilus became a famous person in medieval literature. From the Homeric young stripling cut off before his time, he becomes a chief hero of the Trojan army. Dares states that he was no less valiant than Hector. Benoît de Sainte-

[1] H. E. Rollins, "The Troilus and Cressida Story," P.M.L.A., Vol. 32, p. 418, footnote.

More's *Roman de Troie* and his translator, Guido delle Colonne, did little to change the character of Dares' Troilus. But in Boccaccio's *Filostrato* the love affair is of chief interest. He is all heart and emotion, languishing of love; and when his Cressida proves faithless, he is bereft of strength and sinks beneath the violence of his passion. In Benoît de Sainte-More he passes quickly from sorrow to contempt, and expresses the disdain of the one who has wounded him, with the bitter irony of one whose heart has been hardened, and his head made wiser by his experiences with an unfaithful lady-love. In Shakespeare both phases of the man are united — the plaintive wail of a wretched lover, and the desperate warrior who rushes madly into the fight to cure himself of his infatuation.

Ulysses (*a*), called *Odysseus* by the Greeks, was the most wily and subtle of the leaders in the Trojan War. According to Homer, he was a son of Laërtes and Anticlea, and was married to Penelope, daughter of Icarius, by whom he had a son Telemachus. Even at an early age he was distinguished for his courage, his knowledge of navigation, his eloquence and skill as a negotiator. During the siege of Troy, he exhibited himself not only as a valiant and undaunted warrior, but also as a cunning spy and a prudent, tactful, and eloquent negotiator. He was one of the heroes concealed in the belly of the wooden horse. When the horse was opened, he and Menelaus were the first to jump out and hasten to the house of Deiphobus where the terrible struggle took place.

(*b*) Ulysses is perhaps the least caricatured of the Greek chieftains. To be sure, as a Middle Age creation, he has lost Homeric dignity, yet in spite of the petty intrigues, he escapes being wholly debased. Even Thersites, though he calls him "dog-fox," entertains for him and for Nestor considerable respect. Ulysses is still the brain of the Greek army; he perceives that discipline has grown lax, he suggests the substitution of Ajax for Achilles in the combat with Hector, and the scheme for rousing Achilles by direct snubs. Moreover, he is the only one of the Greek chiefs who sees Cressida for what she is, when she is delivered as a hostage. It is evident that Ulysses, in a sense, is the sage of the play, and is largely responsible for what seriousness it possesses. Richard Grant White,[1] captivated by the ornate rhetoric, contends that

[1] R. G. White: "On Reading Shakespeare."

Ulysses is not only the hero of the play, but Shakespeare himself. Ulysses, he asserts, is the mouthpiece for Shakespeare's mature wisdom of men and their motives. George Brandes [1] thinks that Ulysses is "*intended* to represent the wise man of the play," but really "is as trivial of mind as the rest," and is not "one whit more sublime than the fools with whom he plays" — a criticism which if tempered with a higher opinion of his intelligence, would seem to be more reliable than White's glorification.

[1] George Brandes: *William Shakespeare.*

APPENDIX B

EXCERPTS FROM CAXTON'S *RECUYELL OF THE HISTORYES OF TROYE*[1]

"This triewes duryng, the Kynge thoas was deliveryd in the stede of Anthenor . . . Calcas, that by the commandement of Apollyn had lefte the trioans, had a passing fayr doughter and wyse, named briseyda Chaucer in his booke that he made of Troylus named her creseydy. For whiche doughter he prayd to kynge Agamenon, and to the other prynces that they woalde requyre the kyng pryant to sende briseyda to hym. They prayde ynow to king pryant at the Instance of calcas But the troians blamed sore calcas, and callid hym evyll and fals traytre And worthy to dye that had lefte hys owne lande and his naturell lord for to goo into the companye of his mortall enemyes: Alleway at the petyticion of the grekes, the king pryant sente briseyda to her fader.

"Telamon Ayax that was sone of kynge thelamon and exione And was cosyn germayn of hector and of his brethren whiche was wyse & vayllyant whiche addressid hym ayenst hector & deliveryd to hym a grete assault And hector to hym as they that were valyant bothe two and as they were fightying they spak togeder And therby hector knewe that he was his cosyn germaine sone of his aunte And than hector for curtoisye embraced hym in his armes and made hym grete chiere And offrid to hym to do all his playsir yf he desired ony thynge of hym And prayed hym that he wolde come to troye with hym for to see hys lignage of hys modern syde. But . . . Thelamon . . . sayde that he wolde not goo at thys tyme. But prayd to hector . . . that he wolde . . . do cesse the battaill for that day. . . . The unhappy Hector accorded to hym his requeste . . . than had the troians begonne to putte fyre in the shippes of the grekes and had alle brente hym ne had hector callyd them fro thens wherof the troians were sorry of the rappeel this was the cause wherfore the troians lost . . . to the whiche they myght never after atteyne ne come for fortune was to them contrarye: And therefore virgile sayth Non est

[1] Edited by Oscar Sommer [Nutt] 1895, Book III.

misericordia in bello That is to say ther is no mercy in bataill. A man ought not to talk misericorde But take the victorye who may gete hit.

"The trews durying hector wente hym on a day unto the tentes of the Grekes. And Achylles behelde hym gladly for as moche as he had never seen hym unarme. And at the requeste of Achylles Hector wente in to hys tente. And as they spack to geder of many thynge Achylles sayde to hector I have grete playsir to see the unarmed for as moche as I had never seen the to fore. But yet I shall have more playsir whan the day shall come that thou shalt dye of my hande Whyche thynge I moste desire. For I knowe the to be moche stronge. And I have often tymes provyd hit unto the effusion of my blood whereof I hafe grete Anger. And yet have I more grete sorowe for as moche as thou slewest Patroclus hym that I moste lovyd of the world. Than thou mayste beleeve for certayn that before thys yere be past his deth shall be avengyd upon the By my hande And also I wote well that thou desirest to slee me Hector answerd and sayde Achilles yf I desire thy deth mervaylle the nothynge therof. For as moche as thou deservest to be myn enemye mortall Thou art come in to our lande for to destroye me and myne. I wyll well that thou knowe that thy wordes fere me nothynge at all But yet I have hope that . . . yf I lyve And my swerde faylle me not That thou dye of myn handes. Not thou allonely but alle the moste grettest of the Grekes: For amonge you ye have enterprysid a grete folye. And . . . I am assewrid that thou shalt dye of my hande Er I shall dye by thyne. And yf thou wene that thou be so stronge . . . make hit so that alle the barons of thyn ooste promise and accorde that we fighte body ayenst body. And yf hit happen that thou vaynquysshe me that my frendes and I shall be bannysshid oute of this royame and we shalle leve hit unto the Grekes And therof I shall leve good plegge And herein thou mayste prouffite to many other . . . And yf hit happen that I vaynquysshe the make that alle they of this ooste departe hens And suffre us to lyve in pees Achilles achauffid hym sore with these wordes And offeryd hym to doo this batayll and gaf to hector his gayge which hector toke and resseyvyd glady, etc.

"Whan Agamemnon knew of this . . . bargayn He wente hym hastely unto the tente of Achylles with a grete companye of noblemen. Whiche wolde in no wise accorde ne agree to this battayll . . . And the troians sayden in lykewyse Save only the kynge pryant that wolde gladly agreed. . . . Thus was the champ broken.

"Whan Troylus knewe certaynly that breseyda shold be sente to her fader he made grete sorowe. For she was his soverain lady of love. And in semblable wyse breseyda lovyd strongly Troylus. And she made also the grettest sorowe of the world for to leve her soverayn lord in love Ther was never so moche sorowe made betwene two lovers at their departying Who that lyste to here of alle theyr love late hym rede the booke of troyllus that Chawcer made wherin he shall fynde the storye hool whiche were to longe to wryte here But fynably breseyda was ledde unto the grekes whome they receyved honourably Amonge them was diomedes that anone was enflamed with the love of breyseyda whan he sawe her so fayr And in ridyng by her side he shewid her alle his corage And made to her many promesses and specially desired her love And than whan she knewe the corage of diomedes she excused her sayng that she wolde not agree to hym ne reffuse hym at that tyme. For her herte was not disposed at that tyme to answere otherwyse Of this answere Dyomedes had grete Joye. For as moche as he was not reffusid utterly And he accompanyed her unto the tente of her fader. And holpe her doun of her hors And toke fro her one of her glovys that she helde in her handes And she souffryd hym swetely. Calcas receyvyd her wyth grete Joye. . . . The comyng of breseyda plesid moche to alle the grekes. And they cam theder and fested her And demaunded of her tydinges of Troye. . . . And she sayd unto hem as moche as she knewe curtoysly. Than alle the grettest that were there promysyd her to kepe her and holde her as dere as her daughter. And than eche man wente in to hys owne Tente And there was none of hem but that gaf to her a Jewell . . . and than hit plesid her well to abide and dwell wyth the grekes and forgate anone the noble cyte of Troye and the love of the noble troyllus O how sone is the purpos of a woman chaungid and torned certes more sonner than a man can saie or thinke Now late had breseyda blamed her fader of the vyce of trayson whiche she herself exersised in forgetying her contre and her trewe frende troyllus, etc.

". . . dyomedes . . . fought with troillous at his comyng and smote hym doun and toke hys horse and sente hit to bresayda. And dyde to saye to her by his servant that hit was troyllus horse her love that he had beten hym by his prowesse and prayd her fro thanforth on that she wold holde hym for her love and frende etc.

"Breseyda had grete Joye of these tydinges and sayd to the servaunt that he shold saye unto his lord that she myght not hate hym that wyth so good herte lovyd her Whan Diomedes knewe the answer he was right joyous and threstid in amonge his enemeyes. But the troians . . . maad the grekes to goo aback and recule unto their tentes. . . .

"Diomedes suffred grete mysease for the love of breseida and myght not ete ne reste for thynkying on her. And requyred her many tymes of her love. And she answerd hym right wysely gyvng hym hope wythoute certaynte of ony poynte by the whiche dyomedes was enflamed of alle poyntes in her love.

"Diomedes and troyllus Justed togeder . . . and wythoute faylle eche of them had slayn other yf menelaus had not come and departid them . . . But the sayd troyllus . . . slewe many grekes.

"Afore that Achylles entered into the batayl he assembled his Myrmidons, and prayed them that they wold intend to none other thyng but to enclose Troyllus, and to hold hym without flying tyll he came, and that he wold not be far from them. And they promised hym that they so wold. And he thronged into the batayl. And on the other side came Troyllus, that began to flee and beat down all them that he caught, and dyd so much, that about myd-day he put the Grekes to flight; then the Myrmidons (that were two thousand fighting men, and had not forgot the commandement of theyr lord) thrust in among the troians, and recovered the field. And as they held them togeder, and sough no man but troyllus, they found him that he fought strongly, and was enclosid on all parts, but he slew and wounded many. And as he was allonly among them, and had no man to succour hym, they slew hys horse, and hurt hym in many places, and plucked off hys head helm, and hys coyf of iron, and he defendid hym in the best manere he cold. Then came on Achylles, when he saw troyllus alle naked, and ran upon hym yn a rage, and smote off hys head, and caste yt under the feet of his hors, and toke the body and bound yt to the tayl of hys hors, and so drew yt after hym throughout the ooste.

"Andrometha sawe that nyght a marvallous vysion. And her semed yf hector wente that day folowying to the battayle he shold be slayn. And she, that had grete fere and drede of her husbond, wepyng, sayd to hym, prayng hym that he wold not goo to the batayl that day: Whereof hector blamed his wyf saying that men shold not beleeve ne gyve fayth to drems, and wold not abyde nor tarye therfore. When hyt was in the mornyng, Andrometha wente unto the kynge pryant and to the quene and tolde to them the veryte of her vysion; and prayed to them wyth alle her herte that they wold doo so moche to hector, that he shold not that day go the bataylle, etc. . . . And the king priant sente to hector that he shold kepe hym well for that day fro goyng to batayll. Wherfore hector was angry, and sayd to his wyfe many wordes reprochable as he that knewe well that this defence cam by her requeste how be hyt . . . he armed hym. With this poynt cam upon them the quene hecuba, & the quene helayne and the susters of hector And they kneled doun tofore his feet, and prayed him with wepyng teerys that he wold doo of his harnoys, and unarme hym But never wold he doo hit for her prayers, but descended from the palays thus Armed as he was, and toke hys hors, and wold have goon to bataylle. But . . . the kinge priant can rennyng anone and toke hym by the brydell and sayd to hym so many thynges of one and other, that he maad hym to retorne but in no wyse he wold not unarm hym," and later, as Caxton relates, "wente hym to the batayll that hys fader knewe not of. . . .

"Whan Achylles sawe that hector slewe thus the nobles of Greece, and so many other that it was mervall to beholde . . . he ranne upon hym marvaylously . . . but hector caste to hym a darte so fiersly, and made him a wounde in his thye: and than Achyles yssued out of the batayll, and toke a gret spere in purpose to slee hector, yf he myght mete hym. . . . Hector had taken a moche noble baron of grece, moche queyntly and rychely armed. And, for to lede hym oute of the ooste at his ease, had caste his shelde behynd him at his backe and had lefte his breste discoverte and as he was in thys poynte and tooke none hede of Achylles, that cam pryvely unto hym, and putte hys spere wythin his body. And Hector fyll doun dede to the ground.

"Whan hector was ded and his body borne in to the cyte ther is no tonge that cude expresse the sorowe that was maad in the cyte . . . ther was none but he hade lever to have loste his owen sone than hym. And they sayd that from thensforth they had loste alle hope and truste of deffence. . . . Than whan the kynge pryant sawe hym he fyll down a swowne . . . and was as ded for sorowe . . . what myght men saye of the sorowe that his moder the quene made and after hys susters. O what sorowe maad hys wyf Certes there can no man expresse alle the lamentacions that there were maad."

APPENDIX C

VERSIFICATION

The student should understand in approaching the following explanation of some of Shakespeare's metrical effects that the poet himself did not compose his verses by a similar analytic process. In writing a given passage, he did not say to himself, "Go too, now, I will place a caesura between the third and fourth foot of the first line; I will use a feminine ending in the next line; I will break up the march of regular blank verse in succeeding lines by varying the stresses, use a weak ending here and a broken line here, and round off the passage with a rhymed couplet." If he had paused for such analyses, he never would have finished the play for which his company was pressing him. He wrote his lines for delivery in Elizabethan theaters, not for analysis in high school or college classrooms.

The analysis of Shakespeare's meter, then, is something adventitious which we impose upon his lines in a vain endeavor to comprehend the range and variety of his extraordinary musical instrument. Because he commanded a greater vocabulary than any other writer in the whole annals of literature, and because he was a poetic as well as a dramatic genius, he had little difficulty in suiting the vocabulary to the character, or "the action to the word and the word to the action." Shakespeare's lines should be studied, then, not only for their musical, but also for their dramatic values. As Granville-Barker has admirably said:

> "The elemental oratory of his verse needs for its speaking a sense of rhythm that asks no help of strict rule. Shakespeare is so secure . . . in the spirit of its laws that the letter may go. He does not commonly stray far. A caesura may fall oddly or there may be none distinguishable; a syllable or so may splash over at the end. Dramatic emphasis is the thing, first and last; to get that right he will sacrifice strict meter — yet never music — grammar now and then, and at a pinch, if need be, sheer sense too."

For example let us note Granville-Barker's analysis of this passage from *Antony and Cleopatra* in which Antony is exploding in wrath on seeing Thyreus kissing Cleopatra's hand:

"Approach there! Ah, you kite! Now, gods and devils!
Authority melts from me: of late, when I cried 'Ho!',
Like boys unto a muss, kings would start forth,
And cry, 'Your will?' Have you no ears?
I am Antony yet. Take hence this Jack, and whip him"
(i. 13. 89–93).

"Long lines, giving a sense of great strength. Exclamatory phrases, prefacing and setting off the powerful centre-phrase, with its ringing 'kings' for a top note. The caesura-pause of two beats that the short line allows is followed by the repeated crack of two more short phrases, the first with its upward lift, the second with its nasal snarl and the sharp click of its ending; the last line lengthens out, and the business finishes with the bitten staccato of:

'Take hence this Jack, and whip him.'"

Metrical Values

In reading English verse, one naturally stresses certain syllables and dwells with less time or emphasis on others. This stress corresponds to the length of vowels in Greek and Roman verse. When these stresses occur at more or less regular intervals, the composition is called *verse*, and the regular succession of stresses in the line, *meter*. The prevailing meter of Shakespeare's plays is called iambic pentameter; the normal line consists of five feet, in each of which an unstressed is followed by a stressed syllable:

Thou great | command | er, nerve | and bone | of Greece| (i. 3. 55).

One touch of nature makes the whole world kin (iii. 3. 175).

A woman impudent and mannish grown (iii. 3. 217).

This verse form, used first by Surrey for his translation of the *Æneid* (*c.* 1553) and later in the first English tragedy, *Gorboduc* (1562), acquired the name blank verse because it was unrhymed. In the hand of Marlowe (*d.* 1593) it became so admirable a vehicle for dramatic poetry that only a Shakespeare was needed to perfect it.

Troilus and Cressida, the third longest of Shakespeare's plays, has 3,496 lines, against *Richard III's* 3,619, and *Hamlet's* 3,929. According to the recent tables of E. K. Chambers (*William Shakespeare*, II, 398) 2,065 of the lines are standard blank verse; 186 are rhymed, (a proportion of 9 per cent rhymed lines to all five-foot lines), 1,188 are prose, and 57 occur in external parts such as the Prologue. Of the rhymed lines 170 are heroic couplets, 16 are short lines. Of blank verse lines there are 147 short lines, 42 Alexandrines or 6-foot lines, 1,876 normal 5-foot lines, 463 feminine endings, and 104 with extra mid-line syllables.

Before examining these variations, we should remember that:

1. Many words in Shakespeare's time had: (*a*) pronunciations different from ours today, (*b*) two pronunciations.

(*a*) Epicúrean, Cómbating.

y had the consonantal value, Troyans = Trojans.

(*b*) recórd, récord (both nouns).

2. As today many words admitted of: (*a*) full syllabication, or (*b*) slurring into one syllable, especially *ion* words.

(*a*) To see the battle. Hector, whose *patience* (i. 2. 4).

(*b*) And blind *oblivion* swallow'd cities up (iii. 2. 193).

3. Other words may be elided:

Upbraid my falsehood! when *they've* said as false (iii. 2. 197).

4. Endings as in modern English are: (*a*) contracted by the elision of the vowel, or (*b*) sounded if required.

(*a*) *Incurr'd* a traitor's name; exposed myself (iii. 3. 6).

(*b*) The fresh and yet *unbruised* Greeks do pitch (Prologue, 14).

5. There may be various ways to scan a line, but the grouping of syllables in any particular foot is not important. Nor is it necessary to try to force a line against the natural pronunciation in order to make it conform to the iambic-pentameter pattern. The rhythmic, musical, and dramatic qualities that mark Shakespeare's genius readily appear when a skilled reader of blank verse gives proper attention to varying stresses, pauses, exclamations, and other rhetorical devices.

Variations.

I. *In meter:*

A. Extra syllables:

(1) At the end of line (feminine endings):

a. He chid Andromache and struck his *armourer* (i. 2. 6).

b. Now expectation, tickling skittish *spir(its)* (Prologue, 20).

(2) Within the line:

a. To doubtful *for*(*tunes*); sequestering from me all (iii. 3. 8).

B. Feet without stress:

A spur to *valiant and* magnanimous deed (ii. 2. 200).

C. Feet with inverted stress (trochaic foot) frequently at the beginning of a line:

Let it be call'd the wild and wandering flood (i. 1. 107).

D. Feet with double stress (spondaic foot):

Hark, what good sport is out of town to-day (i. 1. 118).

II. *In rhyme:*

A large proportion of rhymed lines is found in Shakespeare's early plays; for example, sixty-two per cent of the five-foot lines in *Love's Labour's Lost* are rhymed, as against nine per cent in this play.

The couplet is used:

A. To mark an exit, most frequently at the end of scenes:

What error leads must err; O, then conclude
Minds sway'd by eyes are full of turpitude (v. 2. 110–111).

Hence, broker-lackey! Ignomy and shame
Pursue thy life, and live aye with thy name (v. 10. 33–34).

B. To point epigrammatic or sententious speeches:

You have the honey still, but these the gall;
So to be valiant is no praise at all (ii. 2. 144–145).

III. *In caesura:*

In primitive English pentameter, a pause naturally occurred at the end of each line, with a slighter pause (caesura) within the line, most frequently at the end of the second foot. Shakespeare avoided this monotony by varying the position of the caesura and by so-called enjambed or run-on lines. In *Troilus and Cressida* the caesura frequently occurs at the end of the third foot.

Troy in our weakness stands, not in her strength (i. 3. 137).

Often a line is broken at the end of a short speech, and this incomplete line is carried on to metrical completion by the next speaker in the next line. Frequently, moreover, the line is left a fragment, unfinished.

To Tenedos they come (Prologue, 11).

Folio texts are exceedingly lax in the matter of line division, and as a result, modern editors have sometimes had to revise the metrical scheme. Consequently, we cannot always be sure that the reconstructed lines present what Shakespeare originally intended.

IV. *In run-on lines:*

The variation that is most valuable in placing a play as an early or late work is the disappearance of the natural pause at the end of a line called for by the sense. In Shakespeare's early plays the end of the line usually marks the completion of a thought. In his later plays, the so-called enjambment, or run-on line, is very common, and the major pauses in ideas come in the middle of a line.

And they will almost
Give us a prince of blood, a son of Priam,
In change of him (iii. 3. 25–27).

The general characteristics of the verse (few rhymes, frequent feminine endings, many enjambments) place *Troilus and Cressida* in Shakespeare's middle period.

V. *Prose:*

Shakespeare in *Troilus and Cressida* as in other plays mingles verse and prose in the same scene, even the same speech. The unseemly jests and jibes, the scurrilous lines of both Pandarus and Thersites are invariably in prose, and the more elevated passages in the love story and in the scenes of contention among the warriors are in blank verse. In other words, Shakespeare uses either prose or verse, or both intermingled, according to the character, the tone, the mood, or impression that he wishes to convey.

GLOSSARY

a' (i. 2. 220), he.
abject in regard (iii. 3. 128), held in little estimation.
abruption (iii. 2. 69), breaking off.
accosting (iv. 5. 59), wooing.
adamant (iii. 2. 185), the loadstone.
addition (ii. 3. 258), title.
additions (i. 2. 20), virtues.
address (iv. 4. 146), prepare.
advertised (ii. 2. 211), informed.
affection (ii. 2. 177), passion, lust.
affined (i. 3. 25), related.
affronted (iii. 2. 172), encountered.
against (i. 2. 190), just before.
albeit (iii. 2. 141), although.
allow (iii. 2. 97), acknowledge.
allowance (i. 3. 377), acknowledgment.
an (i. 1. 79), if.
antics (v. 3. 86), buffoons.
appear it (iii. 3. 3), let it appear.
appertainments (ii. 3. 84), dignities.
apply (i. 3. 32), explain.
appointment (iv. 5. 1), equipment.
apprehensions (ii. 3. 122), conception, perception.
approve (iii. 2. 180), prove.
argument (Prol. 25), subject of a play.
artist (i. 3. 24), scholar.
aspects (i. 3. 92), influence.
assinego (ii. 1. 49), little ass.
assubjugate (ii. 3. 200), debase.
attachment (iv. 2. 5), arrest, abeyance.
attaint (i. 2. 26), taint.
attest (v. 2. 121), testimony.
—— (ii. 2. 132), call to witness.
attribute (ii. 3. 123), reputation.

barks (Prol. 12), ships.
batch (v. 1. 5), loaf.
battle (iii. 2. 28), army.
beam (v. 5. 9), heavy lance.
beaver (i. 3. 296), helmet, the front of the helmet.
beef-witted (ii. 1. 14), with no more wit than an ox.
bestowing (iii. 2. 38), functions.
bias (i. 3. 15), out of a straight line, awry.
bias-drawing (iv. 5. 168), turning awry.
bi-fold (v. 2. 143), two-fold.
black-a-moor (i. 1. 81–82), negress.
blank of danger (iii. 3. 231), unknown danger.
blench (i. 1. 30), start, flinch.
blench from (ii. 2. 68), fly off from.
bless (ii. 3. 30), preserve.
bob (iii. 1. 72), cheat, trick.
bobbed (ii. 1. 76), thumped.
bode (v. 2. 190), forebode.
bodements (v. 3. 80), presages.

bolting (i. 1. 19), sifting.
boot (iv. 5. 40), some advantage.
bought and sold (ii. 1. 51), made a fool of.
bourn (ii. 3. 260), limit.
bowels (ii. 1. 54; ii. 2. 11), compassion.
boy-queller (v. 5. 45), boy-killer.
brawn (i. 3. 297), arm.
breese (i. 3. 48), gadfly.
broad (i. 3. 190), puffed with pride.
broils (i. 3. 379), basks.
broken music (iii. 1. 52), "some instruments, such as viols, violins, flutes, etc., were formerly made in sets of four, which when played together formed a 'consort.' If one or more instruments of one set were substituted for the corresponding ones of another set, the result was no longer a 'consort,' but 'broken music'" (Chapell).
broken tears (iv. 4. 48), interrupted weeping.
brooch (ii. 1. 125), female hound, bitch.
brotherhoods (i. 3. 104), associations.
bruit (v. 9. 5), rumor.
brushes (v. 3. 34), hurts.
buss (iv. 5. 219), kiss.
butt (v. 1. 30), "ruinous —," decayed cask.
by and by (i. 2. 303), directly.
by God's lid (i. 2. 227), by God's eye, an oath.

caduceus (ii. 3. 13), Mercury's rod.
Cancer (ii. 3. 204), the zodiacal sign of the summer solstice.
capocchia (iv. 2. 32), dolt or simpleton, fool.
catlings (iii. 3. 305), strings of catgut.
centre (i. 3. 85), earth.
chafe thee (iv. 5. 259), become angry.
change of (iii. 3. 27), exchange for.
chapmen (iv. 1. 77), buyers.
characterless (iii. 2. 194), unrecorded.
characters (i. 3. 325), figures.
circumstance (iii. 3. 114), details of argument.
clamours (i. 1. 94), noises.
clapper-clawing (v. 4. 1), mauling.
cliff (v. 2. 11), clef or key, a musical term.
clotpoles (ii. 1. 128), blockheads.
cloud (i. 2. 138), "a c. in autumn," a cloud heralding bad weather.
cobloaf (ii. 1. 41), a crusty, uneven loaf with a round top to it.
cogging (v. 6. 11), cheating.
cognition (v. 2. 63), perception.
colossus-wise (v. 5. 9), like a colossus.
compassed (i. 2. 119), round.
composure (ii. 3. 105–106), bond.
con (ii. 1. 18), learn by heart.
conceit (i. 3. 153), imagination.
condition (i. 2. 79), on condition, even though.
conduce (v. 2. 146), brought together.
conjure (v. 2. 124), raise up spirits.
consisting (iii. 3. 116), existing.

constringed (v. 2. 172), contracted.
convince (ii. 2. 130), prove guilty.
convive we (iv. 5. 271), we will feast.
coped (i. 2. 34), encountered.
core (ii. 1. 7), ulcer.
cormorant (ii. 2. 6), ravenous.
corse (ii. 3. 33), corpse, body.
counters (ii. 2. 28), round pieces of metal used in counting.
cousin (i. 2. 44), niece, a title given to any kinsman or kinswoman.
critics (v. 2. 130), censurers, carpers.
crownets (Prol. 6), coronets.
cunning (iii. 2. 139), powerful.
curious (iii. 2. 69), causing care.

Dardan (Prol. 13), Trojan.
darking (v. 8. 7), darkening.
date (i. 2. 279), dates were used in pies in Shakespeare's time.
daws (i. 2. 264), jackdaws.
dearly parted (iii. 3. 96), highly endowed.
death-tokens (ii. 3. 185), "the spots which indicate the approaching death of persons infected with the plague."
debonair (i. 3. 235), gentle, meek.
deem (iv. 4. 59), thought.
depravation (v. 2. 131), detraction.
deracinate (i. 3. 99), uproot.
dexter (iv. 5. 127), right.
Diana's waiting-women (v. 2. 91), the stars.
directive (i. 3. 356), able to be directed.
discourse (v. 2. 141), reasoning.
dismes (ii. 2. 19), tenths.
disorb'd (ii. 2. 46), unsphered.
dispose (ii. 3. 172), disposition.
distains (i. 3. 241), taints.
distraction (v. 2. 41), despair, madness.
dividable (i. 3. 105), dividend.
double-henned (v. 7. 11), a hen married to two cocks, and false to both.
draught (v. 1. 80), privy.
drave (iii. 3. 190), urged on.
dress'd (i. 3. 166), prepared.
dwells (i. 3. 336), depends on.

edge (v. 5. 24), sword.
eld (ii. 2. 104), old age.
embracement (iv. 5. 147), embracing.
embrasures (iv. 4. 37), embraces.
empale (v. 7. 5), enclose.
emulation (ii. 2. 212), jealousy.
emulous (ii. 3. 76), envious.
encounterers (iv. 5. 58), people meeting others halfway.
end (i. 2. 83), kill, destroy.
engendering (ii. 3. 166–167), spawn.
engine (ii. 3. 141), instrument.
enginer (ii. 3. 8), pioneer.
errant (i. 3. 9), deviating.
errors (v. 3. 111), deceptions.
esperance (v. 2. 120), hope.
exasperate (v. 1. 32), exasperated.
execution (i. 3. 210), working.
expectance (iv. 5. 145), expectation.
expressure (iii. 3. 204), expression.

extremes (iv. 2. 105), extremity.

faction (ii. 3. 105), union.
— (iii. 3. 190), take sides in the quarrel.
fail (v. 1. 45), let fail.
fair (iv. 4. 113), well.
fall (i. 3. 379), let fall.
fancy (iv. 4. 25), love.
— (v. 2. 164), love (verb).
fasting (iii. 3. 137), resting in self-satisfaction.
fat (ii. 2. 48), nourish.
favour (i. 2. 100), countenance.
fee-farm (iii. 2. 52), of a duration that has no bounds.
fell (iv. 5. 268), fierce, savage.
fills (iii. 2. 47), shafts of a carriage.
fitchew (v. 1. 64), polecat.
fits (iii. 1. 61), the divisions of a song or tune.
flat tamed (iv. 1. 64), stale.
flexure (ii. 3. 113), bending.
flood (i. 1. 107), ocean, sea.
fonder (i. 1. 10), more foolish.
for (i. 2. 292), against.
— (v. 3. 21), because.
forced (v. 1. 61), stuffed.
forked (i. 2. 177), an allusion to the horns of the cuckold.
fraction (ii. 3. 104), discord.
fraughtage (Prol. 13), freight.
frayed with (iii. 2. 32–33), frightened by.
free (iv. 5. 138), noble-minded, generous.
friend (i. 2. 83), befriend.
frush (v. 6. 29), bruise, batter.
fulfilling (Prol. 18), filling full.
full (iv. 5. 271), in full company.
fusty (i. 3. 161), mouldy.

gaging (v. 1. 43), engaging, binding.
gait (iv. 5. 14), walk.
gallantry (iii. 1. 146), gallants.
gawds (iii. 3. 176), gewgaws.
gear (i. 1. 6), matter.
generals (i. 3. 180), collective qualities.
genius (iv. 4. 50), the spirit supposed to direct the actions of man.
glozed (ii. 2. 165), used mere words.
God-a-mercy (v. 4. 33), Gramercy, many thanks.
goose of Winchester (v. 10. 55), strumpet; (the houses of ill-fame in London were under the jurisdiction of the Bishop of Winchester).
gored (iii. 3. 228), hurt, wounded.
gorget (i. 3. 174), throat armor.
gracious (ii. 2. 125), holy.
grated (iii. 2. 194), ground.
great morning (iv. 3. 1), broad day.

hair (i. 2. 28), grain, against the grain.
hale (iv. 5. 6), drag.
hamstring (i. 3. 154), tendon of the kneejoint.
handsomeness (ii. 1. 16), civility.
hardiment (iv. 5. 28), hardihood.
hare (ii. 2. 48), timid.
hatch'd (i. 3. 65), "h. in silver," silver-haired.
hateful (iv. 1. 35), full of hate.
have at thee (v. 4. 25), be warned.
having (iii. 3. 97), possessions, endowments.

heart (iv. 5. 170), "from h. of very h.," from my heart's core.
heaving (ii. 2. 196), swelling, resentful.
heavy (iv. 5. 95), downcast.
hedge aside (iii. 3. 158), creep along by the hedge.
him (i. 2. 299), himself.
his (i. 3. 210), its.
hold (ii. 3. 197), look upon.
honesty (i. 2. 285), chastity.
horn (i. 1. 117), the symbol of a cuckold.
hot (v. 3. 16), rash.
hulks (ii. 3. 277), large, heavy ships.
humorous (ii. 3. 136), capricious.
humours (i. 2. 23), caprices.
hung (iv. 5. 187), suspended.
hurricano (v. 2. 171), waterspout.
hurt (v. 3. 20), do harm.
husbandry (i. 2. 7), thrift.

ignomy (v. 10. 33), ignominy.
immures (Prol. 8), walls.
imposition (iii. 2. 85), injunction, the task imposed.
impressure (iv. 5. 130), impression.
imputation (i. 3. 339), reputation.
inches (iv. 5. 111), "even to his i.," most thoroughly.
includes (i. 3. 119), comes to an end.
indrench'd (i. 1. 53), immersed.
infect (i. 3. 187), infected.
inseparate (v. 2. 147), indivisible.
insisture (i. 3. 87), persistency, constancy.
instance (v. 2. 152, 154), proof.
Iris (i. 3. 380), the rainbow.

keep (iv. 5. 277), lodge, dwell.
ken (iv. 5. 14), know.

la (v. 2. 59), an exclamation "to call attention to an emphatic statement."
lavolt (iv. 4. 86), a lively dance.
lazars (ii. 3. 35), lepers.
learn (ii. 1. 22), teach, tell.
leather jerkin (iii. 3. 266), a short leather coat.
leavening (i. 1. 22), the admixing of sour dough.
leave to see (v. 1. 101–102), give up seeing.
let . . . blood (ii. 3. 223), bleed.
Libya (i. 3. 328), the African desert.
lie (iii. 3. 162), you lie.
lief (i. 2. 113), willingly.
lifter (i. 2. 128), cheat, thief.
light (i. 2. 8), quickly.
like (iii. 3. 42), likely.
like as (i. 2. 7), as if.
likes not you (v. 2. 102), does not please.
limekilns i' the palm (v. 1. 23–24), gouty lumps (chalkstones) in the hand.
'loo (v. 7. 10), halloo!
lunes (ii. 3. 137), mad freaks.
lust (iv. 4. 132), pleasure.
lustihood (ii. 2. 50), high spirits.
luxurious (v. 4. 9), lustful.
luxury (v. 2. 55), lust.

maculation (iv. 4. 64), stain.
maiden battle (iv. 5. 87), unbloody combat.
mail (iii. 3. 152), coat of mail, armor.
main (i. 3. 373), general.
— (ii. 3. 273), full force.

manage (iii. 3. 25), direction, administration.
mappery (i. 3. 205), study of maps (used contemptuously).
mastic (i. 3. 73), a gum used in Shakespeare's day to fill teeth.
match (iv. 5. 37), "I'll lay my life."
matter (iv. 2. 61), business.
mere (i. 3. 111), absolute.
merry Greek (i. 2. 117), boon-companion; "The Greeks were proverbially spoken of by the Romans as fond of good living and free potations" (Nares).
mill-stones (i. 2. 157), "to weep millstones" "not to weep at all."
mirable (iv. 5. 141), admirable.
miscarrying (i. 3. 351), being defeated, killed.
misprizing (iv. 5. 74), undervaluing.
moiety (ii. 2. 107), part.
monstruosity (iii. 2. 86), unnaturalness.
monumental (iii. 3. 153), memorial.
moral (iv. 4. 107), meaning.
motive (iv. 5. 57), instrument, moving limb.
multipotent (iv. 5. 128), almighty.

nail (iv. 5. 46), finger-nail.
naughty (iv. 2. 26), good-for-nothing.
neglection (i. 3. 127), neglect.
nice (iv. 5. 249), accurate.
nod (i. 2. 211), call you a fool.
noise (i. 2. 12), rumor.

oddly (i. 3. 339), unequally.
o'ergalled (v. 3. 55), inflamed.
o'er-wrested (i. 3. 157), strained.
of (i. 1. 73; ii. 3. 197), by.
— (iii. 3. 265), on.
on (i. 1. 73), of.
— (ii. 2. 143), with, by.
— (iii. 2. 28), in.
opes (i. 3. 73), opens.
opinion (i. 3. 336; i. 3. 373), reputation.
— (iii. 3. 265), self-conceit, arrogance.
oppugnancy (i. 3. 111), opposition.
orchard (iii. 2. 17), garden.
orgulous (Prol. 2), proud, haughty.
orifex (v. 2. 150), orifice.
orts (v. 2. 157), remnants.
overbulk (i. 3. 320), overtower.
owes (iii. 3. 99), owns.
oyes (iv. 5. 142), hear ye!; attend! the town crier's introduction to a proclamation.

pace (i. 3. 132), step, degree.
pageant (iii. 2. 80), theatrical exhibition.
pageants (i. 3. 151), mimics.
painted cloths (v. 10. 46–47), hangings for walls.
palating (iv. 1. 61), perceiving by taste.
palm (ii. 3. 199), the victor's wreath.
palter (ii. 3. 244), trifle, shuffle.
pard (iii. 2. 200), leopard.
part (i. 3. 352), party, side.
parts (iii. 3. 117), endowments.
parts of nature (ii. 3. 253), natural gifts.
party (ii. 2. 156), side.
pash (ii. 3. 213), strike.
pashed (v. 5. 10), struck down.

pass (ii. 2. 139), experience.
passed (i. 2. 181), exceeded all bounds.
past proportion (ii. 2. 29), immensity.
patchery (ii. 3. 74), clumsy hypocrisy.
peevish (v. 3. 16), foolish.
pelting (iv. 5. 266), paltry.
perdition (v. 2. 144), destruction.
perforce (i. 3. 123), of necessity.
performance (ii. 2. 196), indulgence.
per se (i. 2. 15), by himself, pre-eminent.
persistive (i. 3. 21), patient.
person (iv. 4. 79), personal appearance.
pertly (iv. 5. 218), impudently.
pheeze (ii. 3. 215), drive out, beat.
pia mater (ii. 1. 77–78), brain.
piece (iv. 1. 64), cask of wine.
pight (v. 10. 24), pitched.
placket (ii. 3. 22), petticoat, woman.
plantage (iii. 2. 183), anything planted.
politic regard (iii. 3. 254), a knowing look.
porpentine (ii. 1. 27), porcupine.
port (iv. 4. 111), gate.
portly (iv. 5. 161), handsome, imposing.
possess (iv. 4. 112), inform.
power (i. 3. 139), armed force.
pregnant (iv. 4. 88), ready.
prenominate (iv. 5. 249), foretell.
presented (iii. 2. 80), represented.
presently (ii. 3. 146), immediately.
pricks (i. 3. 343), points.
primogenitive (i. 3. 106), right of primogeniture.
private soul (iv. 5. 111), personal opinion.
prodigious (v. 1. 99), portentous.
proof (v. 5. 29), the thing which is proved.
propend (ii. 2. 190), incline.
propension (ii. 2. 136), inclination.
proper (i. 2. 208), handsome, comely.
— (ii. 2. 89), own.
propugnation (ii. 2. 136), means of defense.
pun (ii. 1. 42), pound.
puttock (v. 1. 65), kite.

quails (v. 1. 54), loose women.
quality (iv. 1. 46), reason.
question (iv. 1. 13), conversation, intercourse.

rank (i. 3. 196), rankly.
ransack'd (ii. 2. 150), stolen, carried off.
rape (ii. 2. 148), seizure.
raptures (ii. 2. 122), seizures.
rash (iv. 2. 61), urgent, hasty.
reck (v. 6. 26), care.
recordation (v. 2. 115), remembrance.
recourse (v. 3. 55), frequent flowing.
rein (i. 3. 189), "in such a r.," bridled up.
rejoindure (iv. 4. 36), meeting again.
relation (iii. 3. 201), report.
reproof (i. 3. 33), refutation.
repured (iii. 2. 22), refined.
respect (ii. 2. 49), consideration.
retire (v. 3. 53; v. 4. 22), retreat.
reversion (iii. 2. 99), future possession.

rheum (v. 3. 105), watering.
ribald (iv. 2. 9), noisy.
right (i. 3. 170), exactly.
rive (i. 1. 37), be split.
rivelled (v. 1. 25), shrivelled.
roisting (ii. 2. 208), swaggering.
roundly (iii. 2. 160), plainly.
ruth (v. 3. 48), pity.

sacred (iv. 5. 133), royal.
salt (i. 3. 371), bitter.
sans (i. 3. 94), without.
savage (ii. 3. 133), rude.
scaffoldage (i. 3. 156), the woodwork of the stage.
scantling (i. 3. 341), small portion.
scar (i. 1. 116), wound.
sculls (v. 5. 22), shoals of fish.
seam (ii. 3. 193), lard.
secure (ii. 2. 15), over-confident.
securely (iv. 5. 73), carelessly.
see (iv. 4. 57), see each other.
seeming (i. 3. 157), show.
seld (iv. 5. 149), seldom.
self-admission (ii. 3. 174), according to his own fancy.
self-affected (ii. 3. 250), self-loving.
self-breath (ii. 3. 180), his own words.
sennet (i. 3. 1), *Stage Direction,* a set of notes on the cornet or trumpet.
sequestering (iii. 3. 8), separating.
serpigo (ii. 3. 78), eruption on the skin, leprosy.
set . . . to (ii. 1. 94), oppose to.
severally (iv. 5. 273), separately.
'sfoot (ii. 3. 5), a corruption of God's foot.
shent (ii. 3. 86), reviled.
shoeing-horn (v. 1. 58), "the emblem of one who is a subservient tool to the caprices of another."
short-armed (ii. 3. 15), not reaching far.
sick (i. 3. 132), envious.
sieve (ii. 2. 71), wicker basket, voider.
sinister (iv. 5. 127), left.
sith (i. 3. 13), since.
skilless (i. 1. 12), ignorant.
sleave silk (v. 1. 33), soft floss silk used for weaving.
sleeveless (v. 4. 9), useless.
sluttish (iv. 5. 62), unchaste.
smile at (v. 10. 7), mock at.
soilure (iv. 1. 58), stain.
sometime (i. 3. 151), sometimes.
sort (i. 3. 376), lot.
sorts (i. 1. 111), befits.
speculation (iii. 3. 109), vision.
spend his mouth (v. 1. 97), bark.
sperr (Prol. 19), shut, bar.
spleen (i. 3. 178), fit of laughter.
— (ii. 2. 128), "the weakest s.," "the dullest and coldest heart."
spleens (ii. 2. 196), impulses, caprices.
splinter (i. 3. 283), splintering.
square (v. 2. 131), judge.
stale (ii. 2. 79), vapid, used up.
starts (v. 2. 101), startles.
stickler-like (v. 8. 18), like an umpire in a combat.
still (iv. 5. 194), continually, always.
stithied (iv. 5. 254), forged.
stomach (iv. 5. 263), inclination.
— (ii. 1. 137), courage.

straight (iii. 2. 17), straightway, immediately.
strain (i. 3. 326), difficulty.
strange (ii. 3. 250), reserved.
strawy (v. 5. 24), like straw.
stretch'd (i. 3. 156), affected, exaggerated.
subduements (iv. 5. 186), victories.
subscribes (iv. 5. 105), yields.
substance (i. 3. 324), wealth.
success (i. 3. 340), result.
sufferance (i. 1. 30), suffering.
suffocate (i. 3. 125), suffocated.
suited (Prol. 24), clad.
swath (v. 5. 25), grass cut by the scythe.
sweat (v. 10. 56), the sweating-tub was a recognized form of "cure" for venereal disease.

tables (iv. 5. 60), tablets.
tabourines (iv. 5. 274), drums.
tarre . . . on (i. 3. 392), incite, urge on.
tent (ii. 2. 16), probe for searching a wound.
tercel (iii. 2. 54), male hawk.
tetchy (i. 1. 101), touchy, peevish.
thicker (iii. 2. 37), quicker.
throw my glove (iv. 4. 63), challenge.
thwart (i. 3. 15), athwart, crosswise.
tick (iii. 3. 314), an insect.
tickle it (v. 2. 176), make him pay.
ticklish (iv. 5. 61), inquisitive.
tide (v. 1. 89), right time.
tisick (v. 3. 101), phthisis, a wasting away.
tithe (ii. 2. 19), tenth.
toast (i. 3. 45), a dainty morsel.
tortive (i. 3. 9), distorted.
traded (ii. 2. 64), professional.
train (v. 3. 4), entice.
travail (i. 1. 72), pains.
trumpet (i. 3. 251), trumpeter.
tucket (i. 3. 212), *Stage direction*, a flourish on a trumpet.
turtle (iii. 2. 184), turtle-dove.

uncomprehensive (iii. 3. 198), incomprehensible.
undergo (iii. 2. 85), undertake.
underwrite (ii. 3. 135), submit to.
ungracious (i. 1. 94), hateful.
unplausive (iii. 3. 43), displeased.
unrespective (ii. 2. 71), used at random.
unsquared (i. 3. 159), not shaped or adapted to the purpose.
untraded (iv. 5. 177), unhackneyed.
use to (ii. 1. 52), make a practice.

vail (v. 8. 7), setting.
vantbrace (i. 3. 297), armor for the arm.
varlet (i. 1. 1), servant to a knight.
vassalage (iii. 2. 39), vassals.
vaunt (Prol. 27), first beginning.
venomous (iv. 2. 12), malignant.
villain (iii. 2. 34), a term of endearment.
vindicative (iv. 5. 107), vindictive.
vinewed'st (ii. 1. 15), most mouldy.
violenteth (iv. 4. 4), is violent.
vizarded (i. 3. 83), covered with a mask.
voices (i. 3. 382), applause.

waftage (iii. 2. 11), passage.
wallet (iii. 3. 145), knapsack.
ward (i. 2. 282), guard, posture of defense.
ware (iv. 2. 56), aware.
watched (iii. 2. 44), a term in falconry; hawks were kept from sleeping, watched, to tame them.
waterflies (v. 1. 36), used contemptuously, vanity.
watery (iii. 2. 21), watering, desiring.
weather (v. 3. 26), "keeps the w.," has the advantage.
weeds (iii. 3. 239), garments.
where (iv. 4. 33), so that.
whom (iii. 3. 201), which.
without (iii. 3. 97), externally, physically.
wrest (iii. 3. 23), instrument for tightening the strings of a harp (used here figuratively).
wretch (iv. 2. 31), used as a term of endearment.

BIBLIOGRAPHY

The following list of editions, books, and articles contains the most valuable and accessible critical material upon *Troilus and Cressida*. The more important texts and articles are denoted by asterisks.

TEXTS

1.	Deighton, K.	*Troilus and Cressida* Arden Edition	London, 1906
2.	Gollancz, I.	*Troilus and Cressida* Temple Edition	London, 1896
*3.	Griggs, W.	The Shakespeare Quarto Facsimiles, *Troilus and Cressida* Quarto, 1609.	London, 1886
4.	Herford, C. H.	The Works of Shakespeare Eversley Edition	London, 1927
*5.	Lee, S.	Facsimile of First Folio	London, 1902
6.	Morgan, A.	The Bankside Shakespeare, Vol. IV Parallel Texts of Quarto and Folio *Troilus and Cressida*	New York, 1889
7.	Paradise, N. B.	*Troilus and Cressida* Yale Shakespeare	New Haven, 1927
*8.	Porter, C. and H. A. Clarke	*Troilus and Cressida* First Folio Edition	New York, 1910
9.	Tatlock, J. S. P.	*Troilus and Cressida* Tudor Series	New York, 1912

COMMENTARIES

Acheson, A.	*Shakespeare and the Rival Poet*	London, 1903
*Adams, J. Q.	"Timon of Athens and Irregularities of the First Folio," *Journal of English and Germanic Philology*	January, 1908

*Adams, J. Q.	*A Life of William Shakespeare*	Boston, 1923
*Alexander, P.	*Bibliography of Troilus and Cressida Library,* 4th series (The most recent bibliographical study.)	December, 1928
*Boas, F. S.	*Shakespeare and His Predecessors* (Contains the best analysis of the characters.)	New York, 1925
Boyle, R.	"Troilus and Cressida" *Englische Studien,* XXX	Leipzig, 1901
Brandes, G.	*William Shakespeare*	London, 1926
Brooke, T.	"Shakespeare's Study in Culture and Anarchy"	*Yale Review,* New series 17, 1927–1928
Campbell, O. C.	"Troilus and Cressida: A Justification" (The play reviewed in the light of the World War.)	*London Mercury,* May, 1921
Caxton, W.	*The Recuyell of the Historyes of Troy*	London, 1894, 2 vols.
*Chambers, E. K.	*William Shakespeare* (Critical résumé of modern research on the play.)	New York, 1930
Greg, W. W.	"Principles of Emendation in Shakespeare," British Academy Lectures	London, 1928
*Guha, P. K.	*On Two Problems in Shakespeare* (Contains the best analysis of the dramatic structure of the play.)	London, 1926
Harris, F.	*The Man Shakespeare and His Tragic Life Story*	New York, 1919

Henryson, R.	*The Testament of Cressid, Chaucer and Other Pieces*	New York, 1894–1897
Heywood, T.	*The Iron Age*	London, 1874
Knight, G. W.	*The Wheel of Fire*	New York, 1930
*Lawrence, W. W.	*Shakespeare's Problem Comedies* (The best general discussion of *Troilus and Cressida* problems.)	New York, 1931
Matthews, J. B.	*Shakespeare as a Playwright*	New York, 1913
*Rhodes, R. C.	*Shakespeare's First Folio*	New York, 1923
Robertson, J. M.	*Shakespeare & Chapman*	London, 1917
*Rollins, H. E.	*The Troilus and Cressida Story from Chaucer to Shakespeare* (An authoritative essay on versions of Troilus and Cressida in England.)	P. M. L. A., 1917, vol. 32
Root, R. K.	*The Poetry of Chaucer*	Cambridge, 1922
Root, R. K.	*Chaucer's Troilus and Criseyde* (The best modern text of Chaucer's story.)	Princeton, 1926
Small, R. A.	*The Stage Quarrel between Ben Jonson and the So-called Poetasters*	Breslau, 1899
*Stapfer, P.	*Shakespeare and Classical Antiquity* (An excellent early discussion of the play.)	London, 1880
*Tatlock, J. S. P.	"The Siege of Troy in Elizabethan Literature, Especially in Shakespeare and Heywood." (A standard treatment of the source material.)	P.M.L.A., 1915, vol. 30

*Tatlock, J. S. P.	"The Chief Problem in Shakespeare" (A popular digest of the article cited above.)	*Sewanee Review*, 1916, vol. 24
*Taylor, G. C.	"Shakespeare's Attitude towards Love and Honor in *Troilus and Cressida*." (A defense of the play as a satiric comedy.)	P. M. L. A., 1930, vol. 45
Wallace, C. W.	"Shakespeare's Money Interest in the Globe Theatre."	*Century Magazine*, 1910, vol. 58
White, R. G.	*Studies in Shakespeare*	Boston, 1886